I, ALISON

I, ALISON

REACHING FOR A LIFE OF MY OWN

by

Alison French

with Veronica Groocock

LONDON
VICTOR GOLLANCZ LTD
1989

First published in Great Britain 1989
by Victor Gollancz Ltd,
14 Henrietta Street, London WC2E 8QJ

British Library Cataloguing in Publication Data
French, Alison
I, Alison.
1. England. Cerebral palsied persons —
Personal observations
I. Title II. Groocock, Veronica
362.4′3′0924

ISBN 0–575–04476–4

Typeset at The Spartan Press Ltd,
Lymington, Hants
and printed in Great Britain by
St Edmundsbury Press Ltd, Bury St Edmunds, Suffolk

Contents

List of Photographs

Following page 64

I, ALISON

I

Patches and Bumps

It has taken me a long time to realise that able-bodied people see me as disabled. To me, I am physically just the same as they are. I don't look at others in relation to myself and think: 'They're *different*.' Whenever I meet new people I always have to go through an initial process of almost helping them to adjust to my disability. If I walk into a crowded room everyone will perceive me first and foremost as disabled, but after I have been with them for a while I notice a change in their attitudes, their expressions. They are thinking: 'She has got a brain after all. She can talk,' and no matter where I go, or who I'm with, that will happen.

People who have known me for some time do tend to forget that I am disabled, and I guess this is because I have a strong personality. Although I am basically easygoing and sociable, I can also be stubborn, angry, outspoken.

Anyway, what is 'normal'? To me, 'normal' implies 'perfect', and who's perfect? I believe that everybody has a disability of some sort. They may be hard of hearing, afraid to speak up in groups, or unable to swim. Such difficulties can genuinely disable a person. Disability is not always obvious or conspicuous, sticking out like a sore thumb. Disability stops you from doing something, whereas a handicap is imposed on you by society. I am disabled, but society, in its ignorance and lack of understanding, makes me handicapped in certain situations. I am not only thinking in terms of the *physical* aspects, like access to buildings, but of people's general behaviour towards me — the way they look at me and talk to me, their mannerisms, the often subconscious put-down I get from them.

This really began to wind me up when I was quite young, and one particular occasion sticks in my mind. I was walking with my father in our local park in Watford, when a woman came up to us and, totally ignoring me, said to my father: 'Would she like a sweet?' 'No, thank you,' I said, glaring at her, and that quickly shut her up.

The sooner that people are able to say that *nobody* is 'normal', this world would be a better place. I get sick and tired of being labelled 'spastic'. I am just *me* . . . and yet others feel they have to slot me into a little box with a tag attached.

The correct term for my condition is athetoid cerebral palsy, which affects my co-ordination and speech. My body is constantly wobbly and I have a slight speech impediment.

I was paralysed at birth, brain damaged and starved of oxygen due to the long forceps delivery. My mum was in labour for seventy-two hours and had to stay in hospital for two weeks after I arrived as her life was in danger. I was kept in hospital for a further two weeks, in the special care unit, and spent the first four days of my life in an incubator.

I was born in Watford on August 27, 1963, and was a healthy, contented baby (eight pounds, twelve ounces at birth). Apparently, however, I slept more than most babies and even after I had just woken up people would remark on how tired I looked.

Early on the main problem was feeding, as I couldn't suck. Breast feeding was impossible and bottle feeding took ages. In addition to this, my body was floppy and lacking in co-ordination. Because of this floppiness, I was a very heavy child, absorbing my own weight.

What astounds me is that it wasn't until I was twenty months old that Mum and Dad were told I had CP. Up until that time my mum had been taking me for periodic checks to the local hospital. She was told that, despite my slow development, there was no cause for alarm. She should just carry on as normal and everything would be fine. And yet she sensed something was wrong. She would see her friends with *their* babies beginning to crawl and sit up, and naturally she began to wonder why *hers* was so far behind.

My parents received no counselling or emotional support to help them cope with a disabled baby. They felt angry, sad, depressed — the whole gamut of human responses — but there was nobody to turn to who would listen, nobody to say: 'It must be hard for you' or 'How do you manage?'

They soon learned that they were expected to press on with the day-to-day tasks of caring for a disabled child, with no extra time set aside for reflection, discussion or the offloading of feelings. It must be a huge shock to be landed with a child that feels almost alien to you, and yet the general attitude seemed to be: 'It's your child: you cope.' My parents were made to feel that they were the only people in the world to have a child with CP and that it was *their* problem.

As for disabled people themselves, some can handle it better than others. While plenty of time and effort is put into helping them come to terms with their *physical* limitations, their emotions tend to be forgotten and it was simply assumed that *I* would be able to cope and adjust.

The support my parents and I received was on a purely practical level, like physiotherapy and speech therapy. I started regular physio when I was two years old. I was picked up by ambulance each morning and taken to the local spastics centre. Once or twice a week Mum and Dad would go in to offer their services with fundraising activities (Dad ran the Dolls and Boxes Fund), or painting and decorating. They helped out wherever it was needed throughout my schooling: raising money for the Spastics Society and so on.

Right from the beginning my parents were determined that I would lead as normal a life as possible. The doctors told them that I would never walk or talk, but I have conquered both. My dad channelled his anger and aggression into helping me become more mobile. He made me do things that I didn't always want to do but that were good for my development. He set up walking bars along the sides of the garden so that I was eventually able to walk around the garden supporting myself.

When I was about two, I used to get around the room on my 'saddle' potty, digging my heels in and travelling backwards across the floor until I hit the wall. I progressed from there to a 'spider', a miniature buggy with wheels, and then went on to learn to ride a tricycle. 'Spider' was a pet nickname of mine for a long time — or 'Crab', because I used to walk sideways in it as well.

For outdoor use Dad made me a baby walker, which was a box on wheels with a large handle at one end. The box was weighed down with toy bricks and apparently I used to drape myself over the handle and, using both legs, propel myself along.

According to my dad, I used to practise physio on my doll. I would stroke the doll's hand with a brush, because that was what they made me do to *my* hands to make them respond when I had physio. When he saw me repeating and imitating this process, Dad felt cut up about the fact that I wasn't playing 'normal' games with 'normal' children. It made him realise the great battle I would have to face to be accepted in society, a society which perceives those who do not fit into its mainstream as a threat or a nuisance.

When I was about four I could stand holding on to something, but it wasn't until I was seven that I started walking on my own. Working mainly from gut instinct, my parents pushed me a long way physically until I was able to walk unaided. I was very doddery, like an old woman, staggering from one piece of furniture to the next and clinging on as best I could. I could only manage short distances. The most I can manage now is about half a mile, especially in town, where walking on hard pavements and climbing on and off kerbs slows me down. It takes every ounce of my concentration and I find it impossible to carry heavy shopping home with me as well.

It is only through my parents' persistence and encouragement that I am where I am today. The professionals just haven't the time, the resources or the commitment. When I first started school I had physio every day, but that soon became less frequent and at my senior school I only had one half-hour session a week.

I have never used sticks, as my co-ordination is too poor for that. And I only use a wheelchair if it's absolutely necessary — say, if I'm travelling abroad. I don't like being in a wheelchair as it puts you on a completely different level to everyone else and people often talk over your head to the person pushing you.

Until the age of five I had to wear special boots with steel caps to give me extra support — and to reduce wear and tear on them, as I tend to drag my feet, scraping the toes. Buying shoes is a constant problem for me and when I was a teenager my parents went through hell as I wanted a pair of wedge shoes, the kind that were fashionable at the time. I am supposed to wear 'sensible' shoes and am happiest in small boots or laceups, but for special occasions I try to wear something smarter.

I look more wobbly to other people than I really am. If I am walking along a narrow path or pavement, they will call out: 'Ally, be careful!' They are nervous for me and think they know best, but *I* know I am quite safe because I know my own capabilities.

We were a close family and did the kinds of things that most families do, like spending holidays together, or going to the cinema . . . and we were *physically* close. There were lots of kisses, cuddles and hugs, but when it came to talking about problems, my parents found that difficult. My father finds it hard to express his inner feelings; my mum has opened up a lot more in recent years, partly because of her job in social work: she is a family assistant, in charge of co-ordinating volunteers. It's the kind of work that has helped in her own self-development.

So much depends on your parents, and thank goodness that I had good, strong parents who were prepared to devote time and patience to working with me — and a brother, Andy, who treated me very much as an equal.

My dad is a piano tuner. He used to work in a paper mill and put in long hours to make sure that none of his family ever wanted for anything. Most people see Dad as jokey and very outgoing, but there's another side to him. He's a very high and low person who tends to keep his emotions locked away inside him, especially when it comes to things that affect the family.

Andy is a couple of years younger than me. He and I were quite close as children, and because nobody could understand me properly he used to do most of my talking for me. He would tell people what was wrong with me: 'She's a spastic and she can't help it.' He told everyone that. I'm not sure where he found the words. He was only four or five when he started being very protective of me. And if he thought anybody was laughing at me he would get furious and feel like socking them in the mouth.

On one occasion we were outside our house playing, Andy's mates were around and one of them was taunting me, calling me a 'spastic' and various other names. Andy went bananas . . . 'Don't you *dare* call my sister that!'

Years later, when I was about twenty-two, he was driving my car, I was beside him in the passenger seat and as we were coming down the road to our house there were two little girls staring at me. We pulled up outside the house and he shouted out the door at them: 'Who do you think you're staring at?' I could see him getting really uptight.

I felt hurt and annoyed, but this kind of thing has happened so often that I've learned to switch off to a certain extent. People whisper to one another. You may not hear what they say but you can sense that you are the focus of their attention. I remember when all the family used to go caravanning every summer in the Isle of Wight . . . going to have a wash in the morning, I'd walk into the communal washing area and nobody would use the sink next to me. Things like that I have had to put up with over the years.

I hadn't the nerve to challenge it then. The actual 'head-on' stuff came much later. I used to get upset if I even *thought* people were talking about me. I'd probably seen them looking at me, or whispering. It's easy to get paranoid, especially when you are a child, and I would imagine the whole world was pointing and staring at me. I doubt if you can ever fully get over those feelings, those fears.

It's very strange that nobody actually *told* me what was wrong with me and I still don't know exactly how I found out. Every five years I was sent for assessment at the Spastics Society headquarters in London. I used to call it the Torture Chamber! They made you do awful things like undoing knots, dismantling plugs — and placing letters in envelopes. We would be split into teams for certain tasks and timed with a stopwatch. For the 'letters' task I can remember four of us sitting around a table. One person would fold a letter in half and pass it on to the next person, who then put it in an envelope. A third person would stick it down and the last one stuck on the stamp.

I remember hearing an endless series of commands: 'Swallow!' was one frequent one. Until I was about five years old I wore a bib, because I had problems with my saliva and tended to dribble a lot. This caused a lot of colds, as my chest was always damp.

Then there was: 'Lie down on the floor . . . Stretch your legs . . . Walk properly . . . Head up . . . shoulders back.' My left foot sticks out when I'm walking and I have to drag it along. I can walk with it straight but it is very uncomfortable. Yet members of staff — in school and at the Spastics Society — kept calling out: 'Foot *in*!'

Andy and I are very different people. I am outgoing and talk a lot, always putting both feet right in it. He is shy, conservative and unwilling to volunteer information. In a way, he's been pushed into the background because of me. It was always me and my disability that came first. Whenever I fell over it was: 'Oh, quick! Help! Alison's fallen over.' If Andy was around he was sure to be the one to help me up again. I had permanently bruised knees and shins, but learned to reach out to save myself, acquiring numerous cuts and grazes on the palms of my hands as a result.

My forehead was covered with bumps from all these falls, and so I began wearing a crash helmet. Knee pads, too, as my mum used to get fed up with sewing patches on my trousers. When I fall over I get so cross with myself — and embarrassed. It still happens now if I'm overtired.

When I was in Worcester a year or two ago, I fell over in the main street. A passing ambulance came rushing over and the driver offered to take me to hospital. Mark, my husband, and

I had been doing some shopping and Mark was carrying a big sack of dog food across his shoulders. As usual when I fall over, I felt very cross with myself, and I took out my feelings of frustration on the ambulanceman. Mark told him: 'My wife's got cerebral palsy.' I got stroppy and insisted that I walk back to where we were staying. (We were on a canal holiday.)

I was quite a bossy child, who did not always appreciate my brother's solicitous behaviour towards me. In fact, I abused it. It was: 'Andrew, do this . . . do that.' I used him for fetching and carrying.

Later on, when I went to boarding school, a huge fuss was made of me when I came home at weekends, and I think that must have hurt him.

Andy never made allowances for my disability. We were constantly arguing and fighting. We generally fought with our fists, like any other brother and sister — but on our knees, as I couldn't stand. I can remember preparing to have one of our fights. We made swords and shields out of lumps of cardboard, cutting them up and painting them before meeting on the landing for a glorious duel! I soon realised that if I cried I could get Dad on my side and so, effectively, I would win and Andy would be told off and sent to his room. In that way, I subconsciously *used* my disability. There was no real favouritism but, as in most families, Mum tended to protect her son more, and Dad his daughter.

Like many children, we lived in a fantasy world. In the car, while our parents went shopping, we played Chitty Chitty Bang Bang, singing along and pressing various buttons on the dashboard, pretending the wings would suddenly appear and imagining that we were flying.

We played a variation on this game indoors. In our lounge we had an electric fan heater with a big orange rug in front of it. We used to get up at about six o'clock, carry all our teddy bears downstairs and arrange them on this 'magic carpet', turning on the fire until it was really hot and visualising ourselves on our way to exotic countries.

We continued playing in this way until Dad came home from the night shift in the factory. He cooked our breakfast and then we went off to school, having travelled round the world first.

Outside our back garden is an allotment, behind which are some woods, and Andy and his friends used to go and build camps in the trees there. We invented names for different areas of the woods. There was Bluebell Land, Giant Land (where all the tall trees were) and Green Land (where the thick grasses were). Rather than exclude me totally from their activities, the boys let me be 'watchout'. I wasn't allowed *in* the camp, but I had to tell them if anyone was coming.

In 1969, when I was seven, we began to go caravanning. Our first caravan was so tiny that we called it Peanut, but we used to take it on touring holidays of Cornwall, the Lake District and Wales. In 1974 we acquired a larger caravan and each summer it became a family tradition to travel with it to the Isle of Wight. We stayed at the Orchard Caravan site near Blackgang Chine, a pleasure park with dinosaurs and a maze where Andy and I were forever getting lost. We had bunk beds and used to fight over who should have the top bunk until eventually I got too heavy for Dad to lift me up there any more.

There was a swimming pool on site, and we played French cricket. Every year we bumped into the same people. The bloke who ran the site had a very good-looking, blond son, and all the girls were mad about him. I preferred Mike, who had goofy teeth and whom Andy nicknamed Bugs Bunny.

Just below the site there was a dairy farm run by a man called Ivor, who was in his sixties and really fat. All the kids, including myself and Andy, used to rally round and help him look after his ten cows. If we got up early enough we were allowed to do the milking, and once or twice we cleaned out the shed: I can remember him coming round to the caravans bringing cartons of cream.

At home I didn't have many friends outside the family. There was Jackie and Janice, but they were older than me and the sisters of Andy's friends — not like real friends. I suppose I must have been jealous of Andy's freedom, though I have no very clear memories of how I felt about this at the time. I just remember asking Mum: 'Why can Andy go off and play and I can't?' I don't think that was ever satisfactorily answered or clarified, just left in the air.

I don't believe she knew how to tell me. How do you explain to a ten-year-old child: 'You are different, and people don't like you because you are different?'

Most of my relatives have been very supportive, though I think my parents lost some friends because they couldn't accept my disability or perhaps were not sufficiently understanding.

I might have indirectly prevented my parents from doing certain things they wanted to do. There was talk once of emigrating to Canada (Dad's sister, Auntie Vera, lives there), but this never came to anything.

When I was younger I felt restricted, isolated. I doubt if either of my parents knew why I was so upset, because at that stage there was little communication between us. It was: 'Oh, Alison's having a tantrum. Just ignore her and she'll get over it.' They were often unsure what was wrong as I was unable to tell them. At other times they cottoned on, making sense of my garbled attempts to express myself, and then they would offer cuddles, comfort, reassurance.

I had speech therapy from the age of two until I was fifteen. At first I had to sit in front of a mirror and practise moving my tongue around my lips, licking jam off a spatula to try and achieve the necessary pointedness, and watching my lips as I spoke. Later, while I was at college they plugged me into a machine to monitor the tone of my voice and try to vary it as it tends to stay at more or less the same note.

Most people could just about understand me when I was six years old. Before that, unless I had regular contact with them, conversation was tortuous, which is why Andy acted as my interpreter. It was easier and quicker to enlist his help. Sometimes he knew what I wanted, even without my saying a word.

I remember when we went to stay with our Nan, Dad's mother in Bushey, and Andy was 'translating' for me, telling her everything I needed. In the long run it made me lazy. I'd been so used to relying on Andy that when I began going to school I found it that much harder to communicate.

I did go, briefly, to nursery school when I was three. It was run by a Mrs Varley in Croxley Green, and I was the only disabled child there.

When I was four my parents sent me to York Road Infants School, one afternoon a week, just to see if I could cope with going to a normal school. My chief recollection of the place is sitting in a chair in the middle of the school hall, the other children in a group on the floor around me. The teacher was facing us, reading out a story, and I was just aware of rows and rows of heads below me. Afterwards, all the heads rose as the children got up and rushed off, leaving me on my own.

I didn't stay there long — only a few weeks. Both the school and my parents felt that I was not physically strong enough to compete and there were no proper facilities available for disabled children. I know, too, that my dad hated the idea of anyone laughing at me and taking the mickey, but all kids do that. You only need a tiny spot on your face and it's: 'Hi there, Spotty!'

I then had to go to the Spastics Society headquarters in London for assessment, and it was decided that a special school would meet my needs better. I became a pupil at

Hangers Wood School, South Oxhey (in Hertfordshire), which catered for children with different levels of disability from the age of five onwards, through all stages of their education.

Each morning I was picked up in the school minibus. The school was only about five miles from my home, but because the catchment area was so wide, we drove around for at least an hour collecting all the other children *en route*. A few were in wheelchairs and they had to be lifted in and out of the bus via an electric tailgate lift, and then positioned in the centre aisle. Barbara, the escort, used to supervise this procedure. For some reason she took a dislike to me and always did my seatbelt up much too tight. The driver was old and horrible, and nobody was allowed to talk during the entire journey.

This school was good fun, with no real work. I used to be quite a giggler, laughing at everybody and everything. The staff used to pull my leg and I would tease them back. It was more like a family than a school.

Although I'd mixed with disabled people since I was two and first started attending the local spastics centre for physio, this was the first time that I became fully aware of what it was like to be amongst them, *en masse*. The main emphasis was on physical activity: swimming, horse riding, dancing and physio. The school had its own physio department, which was like a miniature gymnasium, with walking bars, sandbags, weights, three-wheeler bicycles . . .

I learned to pick up objects from the floor, do up buttons and laces, and walk in front of a long mirror. I had to walk up to the mirror, holding on to two bars and concentrating on keeping my feet, knees and back straight. The physiotherapist stood behind me guiding me and showing me where I was going wrong.

There were leg exercises (climbing up and down wall bars), rolling exercises and stretching exercises, which I did while lying on my tummy on a huge inflatable ball. The physiotherapist would position me on top of this ball and I'd have to try and keep my balance.

My two best friends at Hangers Wood were Jean, who was black and had CP, and Maria, who had been dragged from a fire. Maria had terrible burns all over her body. She lived in at the local hospital and some weeks she was off school because she had to undergo skin grafts. Her hands looked quite horrible, as her fingers had gone completely — been burned right off. I remember thinking that I must somehow hold her hand. I'm not at all sure *why* I felt this, but in the end I did it and afterwards I felt OK.

Maria was much naughtier than any of the others, which in my eyes gave her instant appeal. She never listened to the teachers and always answered back. I was still too much of a goodie goodie at that stage, hating the thought of a scolding and, most of all, the possibility of my parents being told I'd misbehaved. I admired Maria's boldness, her indifference to authority.

The two of us were comparatively able and we did some horrendous things together, like taking children's crutches away from them so they couldn't walk.

On top of Hangers Wood School was another, able-bodied school (Littlewood's). We had the lower playground, and they had the one above. The two lots of pupils rarely met, except on the odd occasions when the other kids used to come down and use our swimming pool.

There were lessons in reading, English and maths — and for reading and spelling I had to go to a remedial teacher. They came and took you out of your class for individual tuition, and the slower I was the less I enjoyed it and the less I tried.

Out of school, I joined the Brownies for a while and became one of the Pixie pack attached to our local church. There was a fair amount of physical activity and games, and my dad used to worry in case I got knocked about too much. But I enjoyed myself and went in for a couple of badges: the animal-lover badge (taking your dog for walks and grooming it), and the home-makers badge (making beds and dusting). Because I couldn't manage the traditional Brownie salute (thumb and little finger turned down), I was allowed to do my own, upturned version instead.

The Headmistress at Hangers Wood was Miss George, a lady with a very pointed face. She was warm, approachable, not at all strict. After the morning register the more able ones among us used to distribute the milk to the other children.

Miss George had a long-haired dachshund called Susie. She brought the dog with her into school and I used to take it for a walk around the playground at lunchtime. That was right up my street, as I was brought up with dogs, and all our family are great dog lovers. Quite a few years ago we became involved with puppy walking for Guide Dogs for the Blind. You take the puppy at eight weeks old, you rear it and teach it the basic obedience skills.

We had Labradors and German Shepherd dogs, and each one became part of the family for a year. We had about a dozen in all during a period of ten years, and I always remember it as a very happy time.

My main task was to make sure the dogs were brushed and had fresh water. I got involved with open days at the dog training centre at Leamington Spa, where I met the staff and some of the blind people, and watched the dogs being put through their paces.There were shows, with rosette awards for the best looking dog or bitch, or best trained dog . . . My mum won a prize for fifty months of puppy training.

Handing the dogs back afterwards was heartbreaking: they get so attached to you, and vice versa. When they are between a year and eighteen months old, they are returned to the training centre to learn to work in a harness before being matched up with the right person. The final stage is when the person is taught how to handle the animal — in what position to hold the lead, and so on.

Dogs are an important part of my life. They are always so pleased to see you, and they never hold a grudge.

Working with guide dogs was one way of helping other people with a different disability. It was an enjoyable experience which taught me so much. It showed me that I was able to give something back to people and made me less selfish, more thoughtful of others.

I don't remember learning anything worthwhile at Hangers Wood. We were never given any homework. I felt it was a case of: 'You come here, sit back and we will entertain you.' Faced with a straight choice between physio and English, I'd have probably opted for physio, but then I was not academically inclined at the time.

Not only am I physically disabled but educationally disabled as well, because I missed out so much in my schooling. My disability needs to be looked after and coaxed to help me improve, and what gets left behind are my other 'bits': my education, social life, emotions. Other people just assume that you will cope, but disabled people have to learn to deal with many different emotions, the kind that able-bodied people may never experience.

This is one of my battles: that I was so busy learning to walk and talk and do up my shoelaces that there was hardly any time left for proper lessons and I've never completely caught up. The emphasis in schools for the disabled is on making you *physically* better. Although I agree with that, I don't think the powers-that-be have got the balance right yet.

I feel that Hungary has got a much better system. At the Peto Institute for Treatment in Conductive Education in

Budapest* they have physios actually based in the classroom. They are known as personal 'conductors' and they go everywhere with the kids: into the class, into the home, following them around and helping to correct the wrong body movements. They realise that if a child is going to improve it has to become a total, twenty-four-hours-a-day commitment. It's no good having two hours a day physio because once that two hours is over, you then revert back to old habits.

I often wonder if *I* had had that treatment, how much better would I have been now? Obviously, nobody can answer that. To get that *quality* of treatment, it has to be constant. When you consider that it's only five or six years out of your life, that's a very small amount of time.

I am very impressed with the way that youngsters come back here speaking fluent Hungarian. When you get seven-year-olds with CP doing that, it just goes to prove they have no learning difficulties.

When I was a kid my dad was using similar methods to the Peto Institute, without realising it — things like tickling the back of my feet to make my legs move. From that point my co-ordination started to develop.

*The Peto Institute has pioneered a treatment called conductive education, which encourages children with CP and allied disabilities to learn movements one at a time, and claims seventy per cent of its patients learn to walk. Earlier in 1989 the Spastics Society announced an exchange scheme for staff and children with Peto. Supporters in Britain have set up a foundation for a conductive education centre in Birmingham.

2

Boarding School, Bath Plugs, Boys

I think before you can do something about your disability you have to identify the fact that you are *different*, and that happened to me when I was ten years old. I had to change from my day school to a boarding school and I couldn't understand the reason for this. Why, while my brother was free to stay at home, was I suddenly being sent away?

It turned out that my parents were not happy with my progress at Hangers Wood. They went to see the Headmistress and said: 'Alison is not developing in the way that we would like her to', or words to that effect. It was then decided that I needed to move on, and I went for assessment at the Spastics Society HQ in London.

There was a choice of two schools: Lonsdale School in Stevenage (weekly boarding), which caters for children with a range of disabilities, and Wilfred Pickles School, run by the Spastics Society. I visited both schools and turned down the Wilfred Pickles one as I disliked the idea of only mixing with spastics — I thought that was carrying segregation too far.

So I settled for Lonsdale School and became a weekly boarder, coming home on Friday evenings and returning there on Monday mornings.

It was only after I'd started at Lonsdale that I became fully aware that there was something wrong with me, although nobody — least of all my parents — had ever said: 'You are different.' This realisation hit me most forcibly during my weekend visits home. My brother seemed pleased to see me but he would be out playing with his friends and I had no one of my own age whom I could mix with or befriend. I did know people and they would say: 'How's it going? How are you getting on?' but they were not interested in me as a companion.

I used to cry with frustration at wanting to be liked and to join in the other children's games but not knowing how to go about being accepted. My school was so far away from home and the friends I'd made there were scattered. Consequently, during the week I was surrounded by other young disabled people, and at weekends I felt increasingly isolated.

At first I resented being sent away. I hated the thought of not being able to go home each night and not seeing my parents. Most of the other kids had been at Lonsdale for longer than I had, some of them since nursery level. I was so homesick that early in the first term I began packing my bags to leave . . . but by the second term I had settled in and life became less lonely, more exciting.

My favourite soft toy, a fox called Winnie (after Winnie the Pooh, my hero), accompanied me to and from school. Not long after I first arrived, Winnie went missing, and I had everyone in the whole school up and about searching for her. We finally found her in the nursery. She was my mascot and came with me to sports days as well as going home with me every weekend.

Eight of us lived in a small flat supervised by a house-mother. There were four bedrooms, a communal living area, bathroom and kitchen. My room mates were Stella and Lesley. I was the only one who could walk reasonably well. Lesley was in a wheelchair, and Stella was lame and very slow. On our first night we stayed up and had a midnight feast. We tried to make this a regular event, raiding the kitchen for bread, fruit and any leftovers we could find.

The next morning a girl called Sylvia Touch, who later became one of my best friends, took me down the corridor to the hall at break time and we played records there. She had something wrong with her legs and could only walk in a knock-kneed kind of way . . . It was a large hall and loads of kids were playing in there.

I remember thinking: 'This school is really different.' There was a wider curriculum and more emphasis on the academic side than at Hangers Wood. Pupils were able to spend more time sitting at their desks and working. We had access to electric typewriters if we needed them. They just gave me a typewriter, showed me what all the knobs and keys were for, and left me to get on with it. I can only use one finger.

I started off in Class Five, with Mr Sampson as my form teacher. He taught RE and English, and he joined the school on the same day as I did. There were about a dozen of us in the class, all with different disabilities.

My first task was to begin making my own dictionary, labelling each page A, B, C, D and so on, right through the alphabet, and writing in words that I found difficult to spell.

There was a small library and we could go and choose our own books. My remedial teacher was Miss Lane, who was very tall with thick-rimmed glasses. I spent about an hour a week with her practising my English — and my spelling. One possible reason why my spelling is so poor — and this I find interesting — is because I find it hard to form the letters correctly when I write them. I can see the word in my mind, but transferring it to paper is really hard for me, and this affects my spelling. I get my letters — and numbers — round the wrong way. They all come out back to front.

I can't do 'joined-up' writing at all. I have to print everything and need to think carefully where I'm placing the pencil on the page. It's not always easy for me to pinpoint the right place and sometimes a word ends up between the lines. It's a very slow process.

Other subjects I did were maths, geography, history and, for a while, needlework, which was hysterical. The only thing I've ever made was an apron for my mother — I believe she still has it. Most of my sewing was done on the machine, which the teacher would thread for me, and I used to enjoy doing embroidery.

I also did basic cookery and seemed to spend quite a lot of time baking cakes — mostly rock cakes, which usually turned out like rock, and butterfly cakes.

Art, too. I hated art. I just used to sit there and pretend I'd done this work of art when all it was was a scribble on a bit of paper. It was supposed to be about self-expression, where they look at the colours you use and the shapes you draw (are they heart-shaped? pointed?) and deduce some deep, significant meaning from it all.

We did collage-type pictures using wool and nails, and worked with clay and pottery. I liked pottery, but wasn't very good at handling the potter's wheel as I didn't have the strength to hold the clay. It was too fiddly for my uncoordinated hands to cope with.

The best bits for me were in between lessons: taking your books to different classes and seeing your mates on the way for a quick chat. I just wasn't into *school* that much. My concentration span was limited and I found it difficult to sit still for long.

My world changed in more personal ways, too. I was starting to become more physically aware, more interested in Boys. Many confusing emotions were coming to the surface. Apart from the usual crushes on pop stars (I was a Donny

Osmond freak and belonged to his fan club), there were numerous crushes on care staff and teachers. In your early teens you don't know how to handle or articulate those feelings. I only had one really *bad* crush, and that was our history teacher. He wasn't good looking, but he was relaxed and a great laugh.

Then a girl called Jenny entered my life — and she transformed it. Jenny had Friedrich's ataxia, a condition which slowly attacks your whole body, starting in the feet and working upwards, affecting co-ordination. Because she had come from an able-bodied school, her outlook and attitudes were very different from mine — and that was what fascinated me. Jenny had experienced the outside world — boyfriends, youth clubs, a full social life — and this was what *I* longed to do. She was kicking against having to come to a special school. She was also instrumental in bringing out my own rebellious streak.

She was a slim, attractive girl with long, shoulder-length hair. She was into bikes and leather jackets and liked to think of herself as a greaser. How I envied her her platform shoes! Jenny took over my life. She used to lead me on, forever dreaming up naughty ideas and getting into trouble, while I would be a couple of steps behind her, generally acting as 'lookout'.

In our final year the staff reluctantly let us share a bedroom. One night we sneaked into the bathroom, jammed all the plugs into the sinks and baths and flooded the place. I used to get cold feet on these occasions and I'd say: 'Jenny, I don't think we should do this.' But she would say: 'Come on, it's good fun. They'll never know it's us, Alison.' But they always did, however passionately we denied it later.

Although I worried about being found out, what frightened me even more was the prospect of losing face, or being thought 'chicken'.

After the bathroom episode we were summoned to the Headmaster, but in his absence we had to see the Deputy Head, Mr Fletcher. He was the one whom everybody dreaded facing. He was middle-aged with a thick black beard, jet black hair and a permanently fierce expression. 'If you do that again,' he growled, 'I will tell your parents and you won't be allowed to share a room any more.'

The thought of my parents being informed kept me in line for a while, but it didn't bother Jenny . . .

In each room there was an intercom system, which was permanently switched on in case anyone needed to call for assistance during the night. Some children were unable even to turn over in their sleep; others needed help in going to the toilet.

Now and again Jenny and I would forget about the intercom and start slagging off a teacher or member of staff, realising too late that they must have heard every word. We were often told off for bad language.

Once, Jenny decided to make a stink bomb. We got some eggs and concocted a mixture in the domestic science room. We let it off in the toilets, which were right next door to our classroom, thinking the teachers would be bound to abandon lessons because of the smell. But they just ignored it and made everyone sit there all day breathing in this foul stink.

We soon acquired a reputation as the Terrible Twins. The boys liked us a lot, but most of the girls didn't. You know the way that girls at school tend to congregate in cloakrooms for a gossip? Well, one day we met a girl called Sally Anne in there. She had a bag of sweets, Jenny and I decided we wanted them and in order to get them we pinned her in one of the cubicles and bullied her into handing them over to us (she only had a few). This episode didn't add to our popularity.

To pass the time during lessons, Jenny and I used to send notes around the class about boys we fancied. We were forbidden to sit together as we caused too much aggravation, so we were in opposite corners of the room.

After lessons were over we were not allowed to go back into the school building, but Jenny liked a smoke, and so we sometimes sneaked into the classrooms and while Jenny enjoyed a quick fag I used to unplug all the electric wheelchairs so that they stopped recharging. Come the morning, everyone knew it was us.

The teachers soon got wise to our tricks and jokes. In the end they let us go down into the classrooms and light up . . . Ten minutes later they would be on the warpath: '*What* do you think you are doing?'

Our maths teacher was slightly disabled after a stroke. She had a caliper on one leg and was paralysed down one arm. The whole class was wicked to her, not just me and Jenny. While she was writing on the blackboard we used to chuck wads of screwed up paper at her. Nobody liked her. She was a horrible old cow . . . One day she stopped coming.

The flats we lived in were strictly segregated and Lights Out was at 9.30 p.m. Boyfriends were discouraged and sex was a subject that was never properly aired or treated seriously by staff. All we were taught was the basic biology of where babies come from. We never discussed relationships or emotions. Most schools, I feel, spend too little time on those aspects and I think that is where they go wrong.

But there were definitely *pairs* among us. Having a boyfriend was a status symbol, signifying acceptance with the in-crowd. Most of us were late developers, and I put that down to lack of experience of ordinary social mixing. We were still playing 'kiss chase' at thirteen or fourteen . . . That's the kind of game that kids play when they are nearer six or seven.

What we were doing was simply re-living the kind of childhood affection that most of us had missed because of the limited opportunities we'd had for mixing socially on our home ground. There had been little contact with other young people, few chances of building up relationships, and so school became a belated outlet for the expression of feelings.

The whole set-up was immature. There was no private place where you could go, no space to explore our own sexuality — even just to hold hands with someone. We didn't have bike sheds to neck behind or doors we could lock. It was all very open and in front of staff.

One evening Jenny, myself, Michael and my (then) boyfriend, Robert, all went into somebody's bedroom and pushed a chair against the door. We put on some music, turned out the lights and shortly afterwards the chair was knocked down, the door flung open and in swept one of the housemothers, demanding to know what we were up to. All we were doing was holding hands and kissing.

We were constantly harassed by staff in this way. We weren't exactly scolded; it was more the feeling: 'Don't do that. It's not *nice*.' This didn't deter us, and we ended up more than once in front of the Head (or, worse, the Deputy Head).

There were far too many restrictions, but looking at it from the staff's position, if you are running a boarding school with forty or so pupils, all experimenting sexually, all you need is one pregnancy and Society would blow its top.

When we were fifteen we were allowed to go unsupervised to the park across the road from school. Jenny was boy mad, and one day she met a particular boy in the park, chatted him up and invited him to our room. We sat up all night waiting for him, hanging out the bedroom window, but much to Jenny's annoyance he didn't turn up.

We tended to go around in a clique: Jenny, me and, for a while, Sylvia Touch. I got on well with Sylvia because I was able to manipulate her into doing what *I* wanted. When Jenny came along she was able to manipulate *me*. The closer Jenny and I became, and the worse our reputation, the less Sylvia remained with us. She was tagging on for a while, but gradually broke away. The previous year, when I was fourteen, I had been on holiday with Jenny and her family to Butlin's for a week. Soon after that my parents forbade me to see her any more because they felt she was such a bad influence. 'She's my best friend: you can't stop me seeing her,' I'd said. It was mainly my mum who threatened this ban on our friendship, but it came to nothing and was not followed up. I would never have agreed to it.

I think I was a bit in awe of Jenny. I put her on a pedestal. She was so much more worldly than anyone else in the school. My parents used to say to me: 'You were a nice girl until you met Jenny.'

My class teacher, Mr Sampson, taught RE and I loathed RE. I think my disenchantment with religion stemmed from my childhood need to blame someone for my disability. I didn't blame my parents — I loved them too much for that — but this 'God' person was just the kind of scapegoat I was seeking. 'It's God's fault I'm disabled. Why me?' I used to feel.

Now, when Mr Sampson started telling me that God loved everybody, that turned me off religion completely. 'How do you know there's a god?' I'd say. And, 'Has God ever spoken to you?' I deliberately challenged him on this every day. I was very rude to him, but there was no way that I was prepared to sit quietly while this man kept telling me that God loved me and all disabled people. I told him I thought it was all a load of crap and he threatened to send me to the Head. I never got that far, though I was thrown out of class.

This is what he wrote about me in one end-of-term report: 'After an early agreement that Alison would at least "listen" to comments in our study of primitive, Islamic and Buddhist religions, she seems to pay reasonable heed and makes occasional valid contributions.'

Neither of my parents were churchgoers, but when I was about eight they made my brother and me go to Sunday school. They probably thought it was their parental duty, but neither of us showed much enthusiasm. Mum said that if we preferred not to continue going, then we should tell the teacher why. So we took her advice, explaining to the teacher that we were not enjoying the classes and didn't believe in God anyway. I don't remember her reaction to this. All I know is that we stopped going and were greatly relieved. It was the church where I later got married. I'm glad it was a different vicar!

I'm the type of person who has to see something before I can believe and accept it as true. I like hard evidence. One of my pet sayings is: 'I met God and She was black!'

Despite my religious doubts, I have never had a chip on my shoulder about being disabled, but it's born in me to fight. I also expect a lot from other people: commitment, hard work, loyalty. I set myself — and those around me — very high standards and I get angry if these are not met. I continually want to do better, not only physically but mentally and emotionally as well. There is always something that drives me on.

3

'I don't mind losing if it's only a game'

While my physical energy was taken up with sport, most of my mental energy was going to waste, but I didn't care much about that then. I was just having a damned good time. It was definitely to my advantage being away from home and having to look after myself and make friends. My years at Lonsdale stretched me and helped to give me a new perspective on life.

I went on various school outings . . . A week in Matlock, Derbyshire, to practise our geography, looking at old rocks and visiting old houses; a trip on the Norfolk Broads; and a week's pony trekking in Kent. A party of ten of us were each given a pony and our tasks included mucking out the stables, tacking up the ponies, feeding and grooming them.

Riding is almost second nature to me now. I began riding lessons when I was two, after the doctors told my parents it would strengthen my muscles. My dad knew somebody who had a white pony called Petite and I rode her for several years.

I need a bunk up to get on to the saddle, but once I'm there I feel so *free*. I can canter and jump and I've hardly ever fallen off.

Like many children, I preferred active, outdoor pursuits to

indoor, academic ones. I became heavily involved in school sports days. They classify you according to your disability, and I'm Group Two. We had running, cycling, tricycle racing, wheelchair racing, one-legged racing, throwing the frisbee and — I was red-hot at this — throwing the club. It was all very competitive and I thrive on that. I know I shouldn't because it's bad to feel you always have to win, but that's the way I tend to be.

I was also good at chess. Dad taught me when I was about eleven years old, and Andy also learned. I played in quite a few chess competitions and was the Gloucestershire youth champion for a time.

I was as good as Andy and in a way that made us equal — because it wasn't a *physical* thing. I don't mind losing as long as I know it's only a game, but if it's about Life, then that's serious. That came home to me during sports days because I can't run well. I hobble along, bouncing like a bunny rabbit.

I remember once taking part in a horrendous egg and spoon race. I couldn't even get the egg to stay on the spoon, let alone run with it. Some of the other girls had finished when I hadn't even left the start line, and I found that hard to take. I was very upset and cried a lot. Somebody said to me: 'Don't worry, Ally, it's only a game,' and it *was* only a silly game.

But in my *life*, if I want something I go all out to get it. If I lost that drive, that impetus, I wouldn't be able to cope emotionally, whereas the egg and spoon race was just a learning process, important to me at the time but not a matter of life and death.

Learning to lose is important, otherwise you don't appreciate winning. I've never been a terribly good loser, even when it comes to playing chess. If I lose, I have to look back and study *why* I lost. I think you have to distinguish between a game and Life. You can't muck around with Life, you have to live it, because no one is going to give it to you on a plate. I know that might sound selfish but I really believe that is what has got me to where I am now. To me, Life is just one big challenge and you have to grab it all. If I haven't got a challenge, then I won't give of my best.

I was never given the chance to sit any formal examinations. Nobody ever asked me, or suggested that I might like to do this. It was never even an option. Later on, when I went to my college in Cheltenham, I took some English Speaking Board papers, and some City and Guilds exams in cookery, but these have no recognised status in career terms.

When it came to filling in job application forms I began to realise what a poor education I'd had and how ill prepared I was for the world of work. Prospective employers asked me which O and A levels I had taken, and I had to answer: 'None.' It was then that I became panicky and wondered if anyone would ever offer me a job.

At Lonsdale they introduced the concept of class swopping, where a class of able-bodied children would come and spend the day in our school and take part in our lessons, and on another day we would invade *their* classroom. This happened once a week over a period of six months and was, for us, an important means of renewing contact with the able-bodied world we had left behind.

Shortly before I was due to leave school it was felt that a group of us might benefit from attending an able-bodied college for a couple of weeks. Lesley (my ex-room mate), Cathy, Peter and myself were selected for this experiment. We had to travel to the college by public transport and join in their lessons of woodwork, metal work and drama.

It meant an hour's journey by train and bus, followed by a short walk. People reading this who use public transport every day of their lives, may think this is no big deal, but remember — I'd never been on a train before. Using public transport was a totally new experience for me and I almost made myself ill with worry beforehand. The mere idea of having to buy a ticket and wondering if the ticket clerk would understand what I was saying, was very frightening.

In the college itself one of the main hazards was the number of steps I had to negotiate — loads of them. I was jostled and pushed on a couple of occasions.

In the refectory we had to queue up with the other students for our lunch, and I had to ask another student to carry my tray over to the table. Asking for help is not easy when you are only fifteen or so, although other people were perfectly obliging and unembarrassed. It was just *me* piling more pressure on myself that made me hesitate to ask them.

By the end of the fortnight I wanted to stay. My confidence zoomed up after being in that able-bodied environment, and I felt an enormous sense of relief and achievement. I'd done it, I'd survived!

Because I rarely used public transport and was still too young to drive a car, I had to rely on other people — usually Mum and Dad — to ferry me about. Jenny and I used to stay at each other's houses (she lived in King's Langley, five miles away), but we always had to depend on our parents to take and fetch us. It's so *naff* having your parents drive you places. It restricts what you do and where you go.

If neither of my parents was free to drive me, I could get quite grumpy. When I wanted to I could be a real bitch, sulking for days and refusing to talk to anybody. My dad would either ignore me and say: 'Let her get on with it,' or come on strong with me, though I'm sure I never got smacked as hard (or as often) as Andy.

My disability let me off the hook. If both of us had been naughty Dad would say: 'Right, you've got *three* to get up those stairs.' Naturally, Andy made it to his room much faster than I could, but for my benefit, Dad would extend the counting phase . . . 'One, one and a half . . .' and so on.

We used to have the slipper on our bums: trousers down over the knee and *Whack*! He didn't like us answering back or fighting each other, but he had to be really pushed before delivering a good whack on the bum. He usually settled for a stern lecture.

Once, when Dad and I were arguing, I yelled at him: 'I'm going to rebel!' — and he went *Whack*! 'Never say that to me again.'

My mum was better at placating me if I was upset, though she would occasionally send Andy and me to our rooms with a veiled threat: 'You wait until your father gets home.'

When Mum was a registered child minder, I used to come home from school to a house full of children. There were three 'regulars': two brothers and a sister, Christopher, David and Sally Westlake. Their parents were teachers and came to collect them on their way home from work.

I hated the feeling that my mum was giving all her attention to them, and not to me. She always seemed to be doing the ironing as well. I resented those kids being in *my* house with *my* mum when I'd just stepped off the school bus. When I first started going to boarding school and arrived home on a Friday evening they'd still be there.

I used to say to them: 'Why don't you go away and leave us alone?' I remember getting rather cross with Andy, as he used to tell me he didn't like them, and yet when I came home on Friday he'd be out playing with them. They were always very nice to me, and in the end, I stopped being stroppy and joined in their games.

Child minding, for Mum, fulfilled a dual function: it was an extra source of income and a job that enabled her to be at home when Andy and I got back from school.

*

Jenny left Lonsdale a year after I did, and we soon lost touch. Sadly, her illness had progressed to the extent that towards the end of her schooling, she could hardly walk and had to hold on to me for support. When I went back to visit her after I'd left, she was in a wheelchair and I noticed how much she had deteriorated.

I think it must be awful to have a disability that is 'progressive' and to *acquire* it rather than be born with it. Able-bodied Jenny had to learn to adjust to being disabled. I, Alison, was *born* with my disability, I've got used to it.

One good thing about CP is that it does get better. I don't know if I've reached my limit in that respect. I'm very aware of my speech when I'm with people. I find a lot of talking extremely tiring because I have to concentrate hard so that other people can understand me.

It's strange, but when I'm out walking I don't notice my limp or my leg left jutting out. I don't even think about how I'm walking and only remember I'm disabled when I happen to see myself in a shop window. Each time I'm caught unawares. 'Do I really walk like that?' I say to myself.

I'm not in pain, but my knees hurt and I wear out my joints more than other people do because I walk incorrectly.

At Lonsdale there was only half an hour's physio a week, but I did have individual work on my hands, especially my left hand: moving my fingers and stretching them. I have little sensation in the tips of my fingers, and in order to pick things up I have to *look* first. I can't pick up paper without crumpling it.

I can't write legibly, so I type on a word processor, though even that can be a slow process, but it's the only practical, professional way of expressing myself on paper.

If I'm feeling relaxed I won't wobble at all, but if I'm put into a new situation my nervous system plays up and I'm all over the show. I can control my co-ordination better since

I've learned about breathing, willpower, and positive thinking — presenting oneself in a positive way: this came into my YMCA college course in youth and community work which I started in 1985.

I used to practise yoga, to help me control my breathing, but it didn't help me as much as I would have liked. On a bad day my breathing may almost desert me and I tense up inside, but those days are less frequent than they were.

It sounds stupid, I know, but I can't bear silence. It affects my breathing. If I'm on my own in a quiet public place I can guarantee that my breathing will play up. I become too conscious of other people and imagine that everyone can hear me gasping for breath.

I have to have a certain amount of noise, and I wouldn't be without my music. Music is an outlet for my anger and frustration. It helps me relax and let rip. I always wanted to play the guitar when I was little, but I couldn't hold the wretched thing, or move my fingers with sufficient ease.

I love dancing, bopping around. In my car I have a cassette player and when I'm alone I turn up the music and sing along. Luckily, no one can hear me or tell me to shut up — because I've got an *awful* voice. I enjoy music to suit the mood I'm in: angry, sloppy, romantic — anything from Lionel Ritchie to Meatloaf.

I'm a great animal lover. It's my dream to have a little farm with pigs and cows, or a cottage with my own kennels. But I love people as well, and that is why I went on to choose youth work as a career. It provides a balance between contact with young people and time spent with my dogs, Dottie and Megan, and my cat, Mabel Lucy.

If I ever need medical treatment — if my teeth need filling, my ears need syringing, or whatever — I have to be zonked out, although there is always a risk that I may go into trauma from the anaesthetic. That means putting me on Valium.

Apart from the effects of the anaesthetic, it's being in a new situation and unable to move into a comfortable position which enables me to control my body when I'm talking. I usually cross my legs when I talk, and I like to have my hands free to move about and express myself. All that is self-taught. So, if I'm unable to find the right position, my whole balance is thrown out of gear. My body is crazy: even *I* don't understand it at times!

After an appendix operation in 1988 I was on twenty milligrams of Valium a day for a week. Even then, I still had problems with my breathing and continued to shake.

When I was about sixteen I injured my left knee which knocked me for six. I couldn't talk or do anything apart from lie flat in my hospital bed. I'd been playing hockey and fell awkwardly, dislocating my knee. I've never had pain like it before, but they didn't want to operate, so they put me in plaster. It healed a little, but not completely and I still had to have an operation later.

If I catch a cold I'm useless. It takes away all my strength and affects my co-ordination, balance, speech, everything. I really do become disabled.

My stamina lets me down. I get tired very quickly and have to watch that. I find it difficult doing fiddly tasks like threading needles or doing up buttons or carrying hot or heavy things. Most people, when they first meet me, jump in and say: 'I'll do that.' This can be more from embarrassment on their part. It's hard for them to judge what I can and can't do, and they probably don't like to sit back and watch me struggling.

That's why I don't like to get stroppy with people. They are in an awkward situation and they only offer to help because they love you and care about you. What others think that *I* consider difficult — like making a cup of tea — isn't difficult to *me* because I've never known any different.

I've learned to ask if I want help. Once, I would never have dreamed of asking anybody. I'd have gone without sooner than seek help, which is silly. I suppose I was too proud . . .

There are still some people whom I won't ask. It's a continuous battle that rages inside me. Once I get to know someone and feel at ease with them it's not so bad. They may not yet know my physical limitations but they know me as a person, and that makes a big difference.

I can do most things now and am generally quite confident, though there are times when I feel vulnerable. When I'm out shopping, for instance, getting money out of my purse is a problem. And if I'm looking for clothes, I prefer to go to shops where I can buy something, take it home and try it on at my leisure. Undressing and dressing in cubicles takes me hours.

I don't allow myself to be hassled in queues. If someone is impatient I will take even longer. I remember once, when I was in the bank, a man was standing right up close behind me, literally breathing down my neck. I turned round and said: 'Do you *mind*?' That startled him. I don't think he'd realised I was disabled.

I don't like speaking out in big groups or talking on the telephone to people I don't know (some people hang up when they hear me), or using public transport. A person in a wheelchair can't just roll up to a railway station any time. They have to book in advance and then they usually only travel in the guards van.

I tend not to use buses because of the steps, and in any case, the driver is usually up and away while I'm still staggering down the aisle.

In some ways I think I push myself too much, but I still feel I could do better. Why is it that one day I can do something and another day, for no apparent reason, I can't?

I hate the thought of getting old, because getting old seems to mean getting worse. You slow down, you may become a bit cranky. Whether in my case all this might happen more quickly remains to be seen.

I'm frightened of relying too much on other people in case I wake up one day and they are gone. That is my deepest fear: to wake up and find that everyone close to me has deserted me and I have to rebuild my life all over again.

4

Moving On Again

When I left Lonsdale School in July 1979 I was more than ready to move on. I felt that I'd outgrown my schooldays, and left that phase of my life behind for good. I don't hang on to the past. I like to look forward all the time.

I had already been accepted for a place at the National Star Centre College for Disabled Youth in Cheltenham. This is a residential college of further education for young people whose disabilities ranged from CP to spina bifida and blindness. Its main aim is to teach students independence skills and prepare them for life outside the college — to 'help them plan for their future in terms of housing, jobs and in feelings of self-respect' (as the official blurb puts it).

I can remember the day of my interview very clearly. It was in January, and belting down with snow, and my parents and I had a two-hour drive from Watford to Cheltenham. The college is situated high on a hill just outside the town, about half a mile's walk from the Air Balloon pub, which later became my local.

We arrived about mid-morning, absolutely freezing, and the first thing Mum and I wanted to do was to have a wee. I found a toilet with no door, just a curtain that you pulled over. This was a familiar sight to me from both my schools, but my mum was shocked to witness for herself such a basic lack of privacy.

First, we met the Principal, Mr Fields, who talked to us briefly about the college and its background. I was then shown around the building by a guy in a wheelchair and saw all the various rooms and areas, including the accommodation, swimming pool and gym. I was quite impressed.

I then went to meet the Deputy Head, who tested me for about half an hour on my maths and English (the main subjects on the curriculum). Afterwards, I had to go and see the speech therapist, who chatted to me about my hobbies and my reasons for wanting to come to the college. They had to prove that they could offer you something worthwhile and would not agree to take you unless it was felt they could genuinely help you. To me, then, this college was just another institution, somewhere to while away the next couple of years free of responsibilities.

Finally, we all entered the central concourse, a large hall where the students meet and have coffee breaks. The sight of so many severely disabled people in one place shook me. About seventy-five per cent of them were in wheelchairs. Most of the blokes seemed to have beards and earrings; some were smoking cigarettes, others were cuddling and kissing girls. My immediate reaction was: 'Oh *no* . . . I can't possibly come here.' They all seemed so much older than me. It was as if I was taking a giant leap. Until then I'd only been used to mixing with disabled people of my own age or younger. I'd felt very *safe* in my old school. Now, here I was in a world of adult strangers, a brand new college where I knew nobody. I suddenly felt very childish, innocent, vulnerable. I was separated from my peers, a long way from home and everything that was familiar to me.

I think my parents were equally upset to see so many severely disabled young people. I know it sounds awful to say this but, apart from feeling sorry for them, I also felt quite shocked to think that I would have to live among them.

I did go for assessment at one other college, Portland College in Coventry, but it was less geared to 'life skills' and I felt it was not flexible enough for my needs, too rigidly work-oriented.

When I received the letter of acceptance from the National Star Centre College, I wasn't sure whether to feel happy, sad or what. It was partly my fear of the unknown. I was also nervous about leaving home for such a long stretch, and in the preceding weeks I spent a lot of time crying alone in my room. One evening I was feeling particularly upset and Mum came upstairs to find out what was wrong. I burst into tears and unburdened my worries to her.

As usual in our family, feelings had been bottled up for too long and I discovered that, unknown to me, Mum also had been weeping over my imminent departure.

Then Dad joined us and the three of us sat in my room bawling our hearts out, not wanting me to go but knowing that in the long run it would probably serve my best interests. Dad suggested that I should give it a term and if I wasn't happy after that I should feel free to leave.

My first term at Cheltenham was a tough one for me and I went through another period of homesickness. Because I was the youngest student I used to get picked on a lot. I became a kind of gofer for the less able male students. Whether or not they were envious of me I don't know . . . but it was the *in* thing to go out with somebody less disabled than you were, and so I frequently got asked out by boys who had only ever seen me once or twice. Some had never even spoken to me before.

There was one boy in particular. I didn't even know his name. He skipped the preliminary getting-to-know-you stage and asked me outright: 'Will you go out with me?' I just said:

'No, sorry, mate. I don't *know* you.' Another boy, Mark, asked me out a few times. He had CP but to a worse degree than I have. It was just a casual friendship and we used to meet in a group down the pub. It was a very free and easy regime at the National Star Centre College. Students could have fairly open relationships with one another, though there was a ban on boys in the bedroom, one of the rules that did get broken quite a lot. Some care staff felt okay about it, and others didn't. At that stage in my life I was quite mannish in the way I dressed and in my conversation, and didn't feel ready for a 'steady' relationship.

By the end of my first term I began to settle in and to let my hair down. To start with, I lived in the main building, but later in my first year I moved into the two-storey Lake House. My room was on the first (top) floor because, unlike some of the others, I could manage the stairs.

The freedom the college offered was wonderful. There was hardly any physio, and more time was given over to swimming, horse riding, hockey and netball . . . and at weekends, there were discos.

The college stood in enormous, attractively landscaped grounds with fields and an eighteen-hole golf course. The main focal point was a large manor house, where the administrative offices, lecture rooms and some accommodation were based.

Nearby was a new block where the more seriously disabled students lived. The more able-bodied female students could be found a couple of hundred yards down the hill, in some bungalows known as the Kennels.

A few of the more able-bodied ones also lived in Lake House, a small house in the grounds which once belonged to the Principal. I was struck by the odd contrast between the existence of able-bodied people down the hill in Cheltenham, and the disabled people perched in isolation on top of the hill, a long way from the shops and town life.

As well as the standard subjects of English and maths, I also did some history, science, cookery and drama. (I played the washerwoman in *Toad of Toad Hall*.)

One of the care staff was a woman called Ollie, who was the most outrageous person I have ever met. She must have been about twenty stone and she was over six feet tall. Ollie became my surrogate mum and everyone went to her with their problems. She was a woman of the world. You could ask her anything you wanted to know about life and she would tell you straight.

Ollie was the one who pulled me through my first term at Cheltenham. Her job was to look after the more severely disabled students: bathing, toileting, dressing and feeding them. I didn't need any of that, but I still struck up a close bond with her. I have been lucky in enjoying good friendships with most of the teachers and care staff in my schools and colleges.

Things began to change radically for me in my second term, when I started doing The Pack. This was a project sponsored by the Manpower Services Commission and involving six disabled young people who had been specially selected from colleges all over Britain. It was designed to show the ways in which they coped with their disability and what they wanted out of life.

It was called 'Who Are You Staring At?' Basically, it comprised a long interview with me transcribed from tape recordings by a woman journalist called Riva, combined with photographs taken by her husband. They followed me around for several days and the end product was packaged and distributed to schools and colleges as an educational aid.

I was the only student from my college to be chosen. The Spastics Society put my name forward as somebody whom they knew to be forthright and rebellious and therefore (I guess), a good 'subject'.

The Pack was a landmark in my life, a sign that somebody was genuinely interested in me as a person and keen to know about my world. Until that point I really had felt *disabled*: this negative stereotype had got to me. I felt I had achieved little and had nothing to offer anybody. Most of my energy had been spent dragging myself from institution to institution, and I felt rejected. I didn't *like* myself.

So much is talked and written about what women should look like: about their ideal weight, shape, colour hair, shade of lipstick. Whenever I look at the front cover of a glossy magazine — at one of those glamorous looking models with pearly white teeth, no blackheads, perfect hair — I think: 'If only *I* could look like that.' But then I say to myself: 'I bet she hasn't got a brain up there, I bet she's really dull.' The only thing she has to offer is her *face*.

When I was younger and looked at these perfect human beings who slid into size ten or twelve clothes, I used to think: 'My goodness, who's going to look at *me*?' My self-esteem went for a burton. For any teenager trying to model herself on Madonna it must be quite soul-destroying, but if you are physically disabled there is that extra, *physical* bit to worry about as well — of perhaps being unable to walk or talk properly like these perfect specimens that we see in the magazines.

Some magazines show you how to apply makeup — how to achieve the flawless complexion — but I could never do that. It's an image that society makes women want to copy, but I really don't know why, because the number of people who actually *look* like that is minimal. But when you are a teenager you are impressionable and everybody seems to look like that except you! I'd like to see more disabled people portrayed both in TV plays and reading the news. I think they need to be portrayed in a positive way and not just in terms of their disability.

My own face and figure bear no resemblance to the glossy magazine covers. The models on the covers have never been *my* role models. I used to be podgy with yellow, straw-like hair . . . but when I was sixteen I badly wanted an Afro-style perm as it was the height of fashion at the time. It took me ages to convince my mum that a perm would be right for me. My hairdresser in Watford has been cutting my hair for a long time and I still go to her. She helps me feel relaxed and the more relaxed I am the less I wobble.

I began to take a more positive attitude towards myself when I met Chris, my first serious boyfriend. Two of the care staff, Belinda and Geoff, were good friends of mine and having a relationship. Chris was a friend of Geoff's from Liverpool. A typical Scouser with a strong Liverpudlian accent, he was about my height (five feet six), stocky with brown eyes and longish hair which he bleached orange. He was always joking, but very sensitive as well.

When we first met I was seventeen and he was twenty-one. He used to do odd jobs: a bit of decorating here, or gardening there. He found it hard to settle to any one job for long, but that didn't bother me. To have a proper boyfriend, someone who liked me for myself, made me feel like I was the cat's whiskers! Chris was a man of the world who liked going out to restaurants, pubs and the cinema, things which were still relatively new to me. This definitely advanced my street cred and did wonders for my self-esteem.

He was the first able-bodied boy who paid me any attention as an individual, who took me out beyond the college environment and who seemed unaffected by my disability. That made it special . . . and unlike the boys at college, he'd taken the trouble to talk to me and find out about my interests before asking me out. We went out on dates together, just the two of us, as well as in a group.

The Air Balloon pub was half a mile away, across some fields. I was one of a gang of four who became regulars there: Jackie, Geoff, Chris, myself (Belinda joined us later on: she wasn't on the staff when I first came to Cheltenham). The only one in a wheelchair was Jackie Fletcher. We called her Fletcher (they all called me Frenchie). She couldn't walk but she used to talk non-stop.

There were two different routes to the pub: the long way, following the road, which was about one-and-a-half miles; or a short cut across fields. There's quite an art in manoeuvring a wheelchair over fields, especially when they are muddy. We used to tip Fletcher out of her wheelchair and carry her.

The return trip was quicker as it was downhill all the way, and we were all drunk, so we would literally roll home. If we found ourselves locked out of Lake House we could always bang at someone's window and they'd let us in.

During the summer holidays of 1980, at the end of my first year away, I flew to Canada for four weeks to stay with my Auntie Eileen and Uncle Evan in Edmonton. They had been over to see us in Watford and asked me if I would like to go and visit them. I said: 'Yes, please,' thinking nothing would come of it — I'd been used to disappointments . . . but it happened.

It was quite an experience travelling all that way by myself. I was not quite seventeen years old and excited more than nervous. The stewardesses and crew were marvellous and looked after me really well.

I also stayed with Auntie Vera in Edmonton (my dad's sister), Uncle Alan and my cousin Denise, who's two years younger than I am. Both sets of relatives took it in turns to chauffeur me around, and we went to Alberta and the Rockies. I noticed a much greater awareness in Canada of disability in general and of the question of access to public buildings.

The only drawback was the climate. It was much too hot for me, with temperatures in the hundreds. I can't stand too much heat.

I would like my brother to have come too — he'd have loved it. He tends to be less adventurous than I am, though he did spend three months in France one summer camping with friends and picking up work as he went: grape picking, orange picking, washing up in hotels . . .

1980 was also the year I went riding in the Royal Mews. I met Princess Anne there during a big event organised by the Riding for the Disabled Association. She is the RDA's President and I was selected to take part, the only one out of my college. About two hundred disabled people from all over Britain were there.

Throughout the day there were numerous competitions and events, and I chose dressage. You had to await your turn to be called, but you were allowed to look around the stables, which are massive. Both the stables and the horses are absolutely immaculate.

In the afternoon Princess Anne came and said hello to us and handed out rosettes to the winners. I didn't do very well but, as my mum would say, it's the taking part that counts.

When I returned for my second year, I moved out of the college environment and into the YWCA, to increase my independence. I shared a room there with two other girls from college: Linda and Katherine. We were collected in the morning by bus and taken back after tea, and we had to organise our own shopping and cooking and generally fend for ourselves.

It was a lot easier to have a relationship with Chris away from college. Belinda and Geoff had their own flat in Cheltenham, where Chris and I used to meet, mainly at weekends. I used to sleep on Geoff's sofa and Chris in the spare room. That was the closest we ever got to sleeping together. I still wasn't ready for a full sexual relationship, and there was no pressure from Chris in that respect. Men never took advantage of my disability. I kept all my barriers up. I protect myself a lot in my own way, and was always the kind of person who would keep boys at a distance and not encourage them.

We were a close foursome and generally went out together in the evenings, but sometimes in the day I would doss off college and see Chris on my own. It was important to keep on good terms with the bus drivers. If you got on well with the blokes who did the town runs (from college to Cheltenham) they would drop you off without telling anybody.

Sometimes I would encourage Jackie Fletcher to come with me down town and meet Chris. We used to have tremendous trouble lifting her out of her wheelchair and on to the bus, followed by her wheelchair.

Jackie and I became good friends. It was a shame that she was not able enough to come and live in the YWCA, though we still saw one another most days — either in lectures, or dossing off college to go into Cheltenham. I suppose in a way she took over from Jenny, with the difference that this time *I* was the leader, the really *bad* one.

Another friend of mine, Louise, had artificial legs. I can remember going out for a drink with her one evening. Soon after we got to the pub she said to me: 'Alison, I'll have to take my legs off. They're killing me.' They were chafing and rubbing her, so we found the toilet and I helped her remove them.

I came out of the toilet clutching these two metal legs, with Louise behind me perched on her bum. Heads were turned . . . We must have looked so funny, me holding a pair of legs and Louise on her bum on the floor. With a little help from someone else, I lifted her up and sat her on a chair. People's faces were a picture.

I have a zany, almost sick sense of humour. I don't laugh at stand-up jokes or TV sitcoms. *Life* makes me laugh — the way that people sit or ask for things, the way they look at me or talk to me. When I meet people they are generally more nervous than I am and I know that I can choose to make them feel as comfortable or uncomfortable as I want to, and when you have that sort of power you need to be careful not to go too far and put them off.

It's black humour. I will laugh if something goes wrong. I laugh at myself when I drop things. I do the stupidest things sometimes and I laugh: otherwise, I'd probably crack up. I get mad at myself in certain situations, like when I find I can't cut off the bacon rind, whereas a couple of weeks before I have managed it. It annoys and frustrates me when I know I can do something but for some reason that particular day I cannot.

I shared a room in the YW with Linda, who was a bit older than me and had something wrong with one of her hands. One night she came back late, woke me up, and announced that she had to go on the Pill.

'Why?' I said. 'What's wrong with you? What *pill*?'

'The contraceptive pill,' she said.

'Oh yes,' I remarked, wishing to appear worldly-wise but wondering what on earth she meant.

'My boyfriend wants to sleep with me,' she explained.

'Oh — I see . . .' At that stage I was none the wiser. Ollie or Belinda used to answer my occasional questions about sex, but most of what I learned was gleaned out of natural curiosity and sheer persistence. To my knowledge, there was never any official advice on contraception or sexual relationships.

As contraception was a delicate area at college, we had to work out how Linda could get the Pill without anybody in authority knowing, so we decided she should go and see the college doctor and just be upfront. Like everything else that went on, it probably came up at team meetings afterwards.

Linda was always talking about babies and how her greatest desire was to get married and live in London. She had mapped out her entire life in this way, and I couldn't understand why she would want to do that. I wasn't at all interested in marriage. It simply didn't figure in my scheme of things. In my typically rebellious fashion, I had decided that I wanted a live-in partner, not a husband. I was just out to shock the world, as usual!

My new-found freedom sparked off new tensions at home, and going home for the holidays became more and more stressful. I had grown away from my parents; my brother had left school, was starting work in the bank and had his own friends. I began to feel sorry for myself again, and cut off from my peers, my fellow students. There was nowhere for me to go, nothing for me to do.

I told my parents I wanted to put my name down on the housing list. All hell was let loose. Dad wasn't at all happy with this idea and wanted to carry on protecting me, but Mum took me down to the council and we filled in the necessary forms. I realised it could be a long wait but I knew I had to leave home. I thought it was the only way in which I could achieve total independence.

Meanwhile, during term time, I continued to enjoy myself with Chris and the gang. We were having a bloody good time, living for today, spending our weekends getting pissed and going to discos, and sleeping in the day.

It was a time in my life that I would not have missed, an experience which taught me so much about boyfriends, fun, freedom — and my own potential.

5

Not All Sweetness and Light

When the time came to leave college, in the summer of 1981, I was upset and confused. I'd cried when I arrived, and now, when I was on the point of leaving, I was in tears again! Why should this be? Well, the fact was, I had no job in view and no immediate prospect of one. For the first time in my life I hadn't got a 'next stage' in my mind's eye.

Before I left, the college's careers officer, Cheryl Hambrook, came to see me and asked what I wanted to do. I told her I'd be interested in working with Guide Dogs for the Blind. Dogs love you no matter what. Even if you come home in a bad mood they still wag their tails and jump all over you. People, I felt, still had the power to hurt and alienate me.

We talked and talked, and Cheryl Hambrook set up a week's work experience for me, in an office. I wasn't keen, but she wanted me to have a go. I was sent to the Spastics Society headquarters in London, where I spent the mornings doing clerical work and the afternoons in reception. I disliked being confined to one area and hated the fiddly, repetitive tasks like filing and typing, the lack of contact with people. It was not me at all.

After the week was up, the Spastics Society sent a written assessment of me to the college. I then attended a meeting with my parents, my personal tutor, the careers officer, the college Principal (Mr Fields), and the county careers officer (Mr Taylor). They were all there to try to find me something to do when I left college.

I made it perfectly clear that office work was not to my liking. They didn't seem too happy about that, and my repeated wish to work with guide dogs was more or less ignored. I sat there thinking: 'They don't know what to do with me. They just want me to fit into one of their tidy slots.'

Some form of community service work was suggested as a possible option and my dad immediately sounded off about not wanting his seventeen-year-old daughter to fill her time 'pottering about with old ladies'.

The college careers people were not very constructive in their advice and I felt they didn't care about developing me and my potential.

Things were left in abeyance after that meeting and the onus for my future career rested with my parents, which may have turned out for the best in the longterm. Otherwise, I might have ended up stuffing teddy bears. Ultimately, the purpose behind going for assessments is to find out if you are employable. The Spastics Society have their own centres and sheltered workshops around the country, and if you wish you can be sent there and spend your days packing boxes or making baskets. When I look back, I was actually willing for that to happen early on, as I knew of no alternative.

Establishments seem unable to think beyond the confines of factory life, or gardening centres, and I feel that this limits what they offer disabled people. That's a great shame, as it means that a person will fail to achieve their potential. When I left college at sixteen, nobody — including myself — dreamed that I would ever be a professional worker with qualifications. It was assumed that if you did work it would be in a factory, and to prepare you for a life on the shop floor they train you in practical skills, which for me can be difficult as my hands aren't very co-ordinated. For some odd reason disabled people have tended to be given jobs that are very *physical*. Thank goodness, now the computer age has got under way, things are starting to change.

I remember when I did my first TV programme, *Man Alive*, back in 1980, there was a guy taking part who was very severely disabled with CP and yet was a qualified barrister. I was amazed by this at the time.

What needs to happen is for people to be judged on their own personality and not on their disability. There should be more emphasis on: 'What would *you* like to do?' rather than simply assessing basic individual capabilities.

I hate sheltered workshops. They deal with meaningless tasks. They do not benefit the worker, who is only paid a pittance (about £4.00 a week), because to pay them a decent wage would apparently affect their entitlement to other benefits. There is no fulfilment involved. It's just a case of: 'Here we go again — another day of packing.'

I have been to several such centres and been horrified at what I've found, because some of the people who work there are so *able* and yet they've been pushed away from Society and from the wider opportunities available, simply on the grounds of their disability.

I think I am so lucky not to be in their position, because when it came to making big decisions about my future, I didn't have the power . . . or I didn't know how to *use* my power to be assertive and to say: 'No, I don't want that.' It was only because I had strong parents who had *ideas* that I wasn't manipulated into that system. It happens to so many people, and when I realise how close I was to joining them it really frightens me.

It's an easy way out for people like careers officers and teachers to get disabled people off their backs, and I would imagine that once you are in that kind of environment, breaking out from there is very hard.

Back at Watford, I started job hunting on my own and was invited to an interview with the Disabled Resettlement Officer at the careers office. We kicked around lots of different ideas and it seemed that the most appropriate one for me at that time was YOPS, the government's training scheme for the young unemployed. The careers officer got in touch with YOPS on my behalf and recommended that I be considered for a place on their programme.

I was asked to attend a further interview with the YOPS board, who wanted to know what I could and couldn't do. I found that difficult to answer, as even *I* wasn't certain of my own limitations: until then, I'd never been given a chance to test them! I gave the matter a lot of serious thought and, although I'd previously been drawn more to dogs than to human beings, I decided that I would like to work with people after all and would welcome the challenge of trying to educate them about disability. It was then suggested that I might like to do a placement with the youth and community service of SW Hertfordshire. For this I would need to go for yet another interview — 'to see if they can use you'.

I didn't have much idea of what the youth and community service was about. I felt nervous at the prospect of working with large numbers of people, but at the same time excited at the thought of having a job with responsibilities and objectives rather than some menial position in an office or on a factory assembly line.

I was interviewed for one of four sponsored places by Mike Hockings and Peter Crooks, youth and community officers with SW Herts. They asked me why I was interested in doing youth work. I bullshitted my way through their

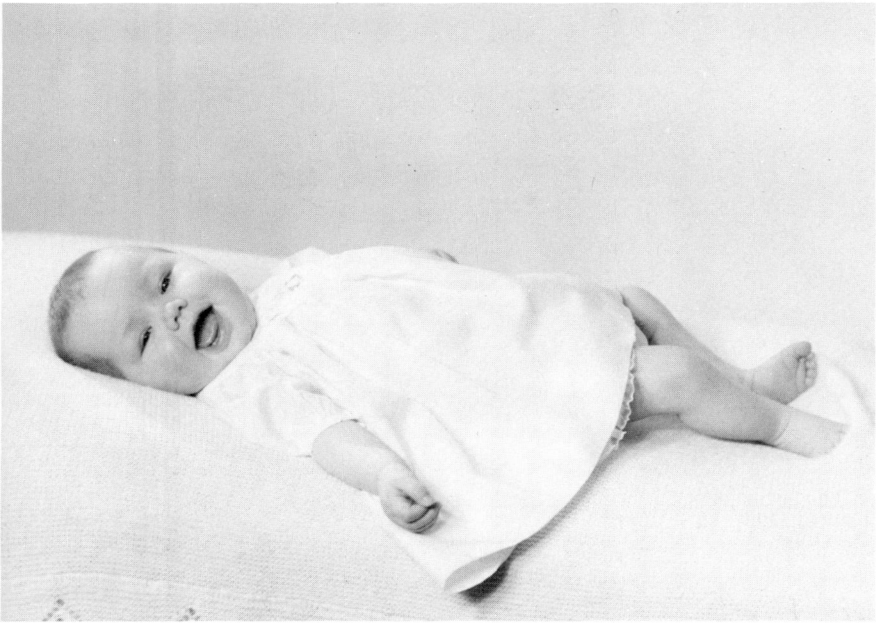

Six months old. The whole world before me!

Alone with the first man in my life, my dad.

School photo day, aged 8. Smile please.

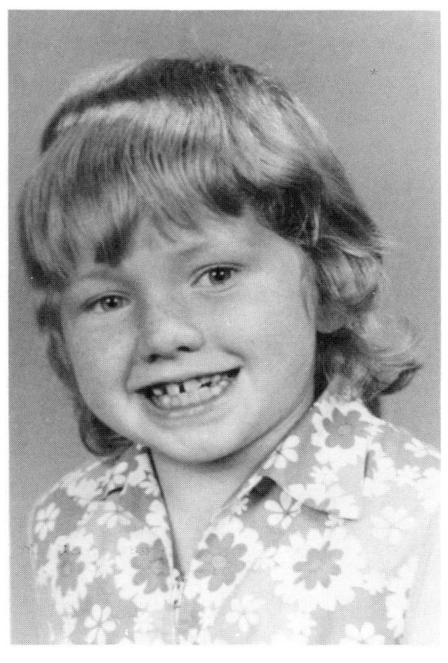

Above: My sports career ended here. I only liked winning. Hangar's Wood School, 1971.

Right: Seaside sun. Mum, Andy and me.

Linda and me in the college swimming team,
National Star Centre.

Being assessed at Fitzroy Square.

My leaving party from the Youth and Community Service, Watford, July 1985.

Philip and me in hospitality after *Going Live*.

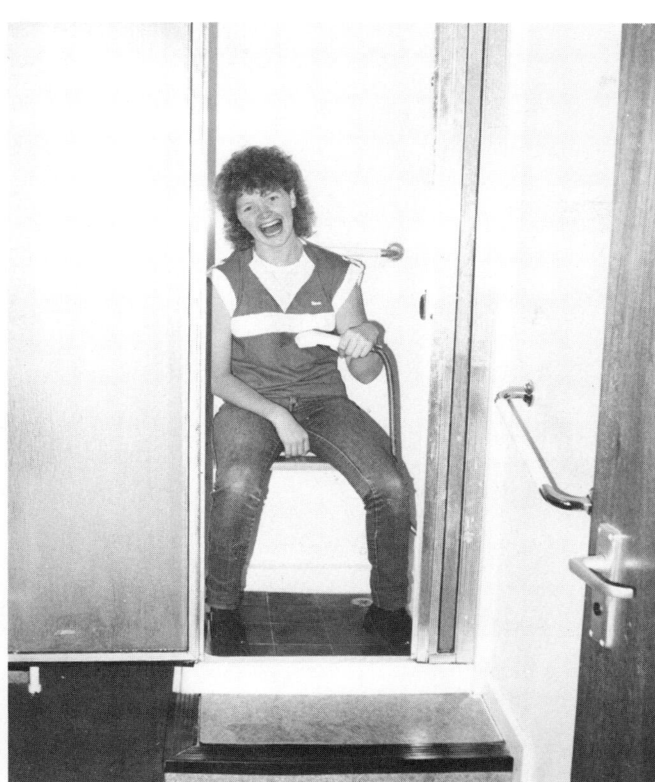

Left: Trying out the new shower in my flat.

Below: Graduating. The piece of paper that says it all.

Rugby tackle! With Mark after a game in Oxford, 1986.

Filming is fun. Ann Paul and me during the making of *I, Alison*.

Giving the low down to the kids at
Gwyrosydd School, 1987.

With Bishop Vaughan who married us.

l. to r. Andy, Mum, Mark, Me, Dad.

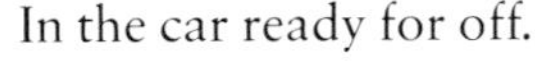

In the car ready for off.

questions and they agreed to take me on, at an initial weekly wage of around £20.00. Mike Hockings supervised me throughout.

My first placement was with a local play scheme for two weeks, helping to supervise eighty or so kids aged from six to eleven years old. Young kids are not my strong point. I find them hard work, and it was a horrendous experience. They were constantly on the go and I felt completely out of my depth. We did a bit of painting and played chess and outdoor ball games. There were four or five other helpers, plus a leader, but I had no idea what I was supposed to be doing and just wandered around like a lost soul.

I was the only disabled helper. Young kids, I find, are more honest than older ones in their approach. They are less inclined to take the mickey. They simply ask outright: 'What's wrong with you?' In a way, that's less hurtful and easier to relate to, though it is hard explaining to very young children. Most of them don't understand. Some just *look* at you and go: 'Aaah!'

As I still hadn't learned to drive, I had to rely on the other workers for lifts and they were good to me, transporting me to and from work.

My next assignment was with the Carey Place coffee bar in Watford, serving sandwiches and beefburgers and trying to build up a rapport with the young, predominantly Afro-Caribbean clientele.

I found the experience extremely challenging, because they were mainly men, mainly black and mostly in their twenties. I was a white, disabled woman and only eighteen. Some black men tend to look down on women and believe that women are there primarily to service them, but these guys soon got to know and accept me and if there was a fight I was the one who would intervene. It's no good sending in another man to break up a fight between other men, but as a woman I knew that I could walk in there and they wouldn't touch me.

They taught me how to play pool. Their language was diabolical! I'd reckoned I was streetwise, but I certainly learned some new words there! They smoked dope — *ganja* — and that, too, was new to me. How very innocent I was in those days!

I stayed at the coffee bar for about six months and was just settling in when it was time to move to my third and final placement: at Cassio College in Watford. I was based in the college's youth wing with two other workers. There were facilities for playing table tennis and pool, and I was in charge of the money, taking deposits to book games and equipment.

There were student barbecues, and I carried out a survey of students' attitudes to disabled people, recording details of access to the college building and how they would feel about disabled students going there. A core of us worked together on this. My aim was to win support for the idea that more college places should be made available for disabled students.

Although I'm obviously all in favour of better access to buildings — and this is improving — my argument is: 'What's the point of being able to get into a building if the person behind the door or counter doesn't know how to talk to you?' It's all to do with attitudes. If disabled people conform to other people's ideas of what they should do or be, that reinforces society's view of them as helpless, passive beings full of sweetness and light. What is needed is for disabled people to get off their backsides and *rebel*, and for society to take notice. It's a two-way process. If more disabled people said: 'I'm not putting up with this any longer,' and *made* society take notice, then attitudes would gradually change.

While I was at Cassio College I also gave talks about disability to the home care staff and social workers. They were quiet and nervous at first, unsure about my role there, but they responded well and we enjoyed some lively discussions.

Meanwhile, Chris and I had split up. We had been drifting apart ever since I left Cheltenham, though I did see him for a while afterwards. He used to come and see me in Watford, or I would travel to Cheltenham and meet him at Belinda's flat. But the telephone calls became less frequent, until they petered out altogether.

I cried over him at first, but I wasn't heartbroken. I never did let anyone get that close to me and I still kept up all my barriers. In any case, that was about the time when other important and intriguing diversions were due to dominate my life.

6

'Why do you talk funny, Goldilocks?'

A new phase in my life started in the summer of 1981, around the time of my eighteenth birthday, in August. The guys at the coffee bar bought me a huge card and all signed it: Happy birthday, Ally. A small group of us from the National Star Centre (including Geoff and Belinda) celebrated at Bailey's, a night club in Watford. We all got pretty tight and went back afterwards to my parents' house. They were away for the weekend, and it was a good 'do'.

1981 was also the year in which I passed my driving test, another turning point. It was decided that I needed to drive, to give me greater independence. I had managed to save £500 from my mobility allowance to buy a second-hand car. Disabled people are entitled to this allowance if they can't walk long distances or use public transport. Mum, Dad and I shopped around various dealers until we found this ancient blue automatic Mini. It was a real old banger, but I wanted it!

We took the car for a test drive. I then went to the bank and withdrew my savings. After buying the Mini, I had regular practice in it with my parents. Learning with my dad was chronic and we nearly came to blows at times, but driving comes quite naturally to me and I feel at ease behind the wheel.

I also had five lessons with a driving school. My instructor was always telling me off for speeding. I could never manage to stick to thirty miles an hour and I still have problems with speed limits, but I've not been caught yet (touch wood!).

I had the standard driving test, with an extra fifteen minutes tagged on. Personally, I felt that to be singled out in this way was a mark of excellence, showing that I really must have been well above average in the driving stakes.

It was in September 1981, I passed first time — and it has changed my life. Learning to drive was the key to my independence, giving me the freedom to do what I want and go where I want when I want. It has also been a way of competing and surviving in the job market, a vital asset here.

My efforts at learning to drive were recorded in a television documentary programme in the BBC2 *Forty Minutes* series, which went out in 1981.

My very first encounter with the media took place in 1980, the International Year of Disabled People. The BBC approached me to appear in their *Man Alive* series (on TV), to help promote positive images of disabled people. There were two blokes and myself, all from different colleges, and the programme explored our attitudes to disability and to life in general. The main aim was to encourage the able-bodied population to regard disabled people in a more enlightened and less patronising way — to bridge gaps between these two sectors of the community.

There was such a favourable response and so much feedback that in 1981 the BBC decided to make a follow-up, concentrating on me alone (*Forty Minutes*). On this occasion I was able to have more direct control and involvement in the finished product.

I was shown attending the case conference in Cheltenham held to discuss my future career prospects, the subsequent interview with Watford Careers Office and — stage three —

my interview with the youth and community service. Plus, of course, me at the wheel of my Mini. The cameras were not allowed to film the test itself, but they showed me being told the result.

Again, there were all sorts of positive spin-offs from the programme, including a flood of job offers — from dog kennels, housing agencies, a sewing factory . . . So many telephone calls and letters saying: 'Come and work for me.' All of them kind gestures from well intentioned people, but none of them right for *me*.

At that stage both Ann Paul, the producer of *Forty Minutes*, and myself felt that enough was enough. We were loath to court more publicity by making any more programmes, as the presence of cameras filming me might have given me an unfair advantage over others, pressurising people into offering me work that would otherwise perhaps have been denied me. I didn't want that to happen. I wanted to be accepted on my own merits and not because I had been seen on television.

Ann Paul taught me a great deal. It was thanks to her that I was able for the first time in any depth to express how I felt about being a disabled person in an able-bodied world. Making that programme was an enjoyable experience and another personal landmark. It made me realise that I was a good communicator with a possible contribution to make to Society.

The biggest boost to my confidence came when I was taken on as a part-time worker with the youth and community service of SW Herts. After my stint with Cassio College my YOPS contract had terminated, which meant that two basic options were open to me: either youth and community could hire me as a part-time worker, or else I had to find something else to do. They agreed, thank goodness, to place me on their payroll.

I was now a proper worker with a real job, as opposed to a temporary training scheme. Things began to move quite fast, and although I was only designated part-time, I put in a lot of hours: about four sessions a week, of three hours a time.

As County Adviser to Disabled People, one of my main duties was to visit and monitor the running of PHAB (Physically Handicapped and Able-Bodied) clubs throughout the county. PHAB's aim (as the name suggests) is to foster the integration of physically handicapped people with the rest of the community. There are a number of PHAB clubs all over Herts and it was my responsibility to co-ordinate them effectively.

I was unhappy about this aspect of the job as I disagree with the fundamental ethos behind PHAB. Why? — because I believe that it creates an artificial atmosphere surrounding integration. What happens is that you get the 'nice' able-bodied kids going to PHAB and it is not 'nice' kids who need to be 'converted'. In other words, PHAB does not reflect the *real* world as most of us experience it. I think that integrated youth clubs are a much better idea.

Other tasks included giving talks to schools and youth clubs, deputising for youth workers who were unwell, and team work: helping to organise holiday schemes and play schemes.

When I give talks I work from a series of cards which carry my own scribbled notes; little one-liners like: 'Discuss attitudes — half an hour.' I've devised two basic talks: one about myself and my life, and one about disability in general. The latter also starts off with me discussing my own disability. I get a class of ten- to eleven-year-olds, sit some of them in a wheelchair and make them wear thick, heavy duty rubber gloves so that their hands don't function well and feel clumsy. Then we talk about what it means to have a disability. One thing they always ask me is: 'Would you like to be normal?' I try to answer that as best I can and say: 'To me, I *am* normal, because I don't know any different.' I think they find that difficult to take in. I also teach them sign language (I learned this at Lonsdale) and let them practise communicating that way. With older children we examine our attitudes and prejudices on all kinds of major issues, such as abortion or sexuality and the disabled.

In my spare time I became interested in Citizens Band radio, a big craze in the early eighties. Tim, an old friend of my age, had a car and was into CB, and it was he who introduced me to it. Tim and I had been through so much together, from early physio sessions at the Watford spastics centre (he had CP) to Cheltenham where he, too, was a student. He lives in Bushey and is now helping his father run an antiques business.

CB made me loads of new friends, bringing me into contact with other young people in my area or 'channel'. I was fascinated that the simple act of turning a switch enabled one to *talk* to people.

Everyone had to have a 'handle': that's a sort of coded name. Because my hair was curly and quite long, my 'handle' was Goldilocks.

I can remember turning on my radio for the first time and hearing what amounted to a special language. There was this boy on the other end saying: '1414 for a copy,' which is jargon for: 'Is there anybody out there who wants to talk to me?' I answered, giving my name. Then I heard: 'There's a wind-up on the channel,' which, translated, means: 'Somebody is having us on.' Because of my speech impediment they thought I was deliberately messing about, and it took me a long time to make people understand that I was disabled. Although they could hear there was something wrong with my voice they thought I was just acting stupid and so nobody would talk to me for ages. What I had to do to get through to them was actually to meet people face to face, to 'have eyeballs', as they call it. (Each of you has a little code book, a user's guide to CB jargon.)

The boy who first spoke to me was a kid of about fourteen called Christopher Robin. He said to me: 'Why do you talk funny, Goldilocks?'

'Because I'm disabled,' I replied.

'I don't believe you.'

'All right,' I said, 'I'll meet you and I'll prove it.'

So I had this 'eyeball' with him and he was quite shocked. Afterwards, he must have told everyone else on the 'channel' that I really was disabled and from then on it was wonderful. My social circle grew, everyone on the 'channel' was supportive and they often used to call for me on the radio.

There were ten in our group, mostly boys and men, including Christopher Robin, Conrad, Tiny Tim and The Outlaw. Most of us had cars and we would fix a time to meet at the park (our main rendezvous) near my parents' home in Croxley Green. We'd go around in convoys of cars, each talking to one another as we drove along.

One day we drove down to Sussex, following each other and talking on our radios all the way down the A23 to Brighton, where we spent the day. When you are driving you move into other 'channels' and so, depending on weather conditions, you can find yourself talking to people outside your own particular group, transmitting messages further afield.

CB, like driving a car, transformed my life and boosted my independence. It also led me to Boyfriend Number Two: Ray, a.k.a. The Outlaw. Our group used to hang out together, all good mates with no 'heavy' relationships going on. But I wanted a Union Jack sprayed on my Mini's roof, and Ray said he would oblige — on condition that I went out with him one night. I hesitated, I wasn't that keen on him, but I did hanker after this Union Jack . . . so I agreed to go out with him, persuading my friend Belinda to accompany me. Belinda had left Cheltenham to come to Watford, where she worked as a nanny. She moved there partly to renew her friendship with me and was part of our CB group. Her 'handle' was Nanny.

We all went to a pub called the Halfway House: myself, Ray, Belinda and her new boyfriend, Ian, another CB freak whom she later married (Geoff was off the scene by this time).

Ray kept his word and a couple of days later I got my Union Jack! He was a carpenter and lived with his parents in Watford. He was tall and clean-cut and drove a smart car. We went out together for about two years, but he was too set in his ways for me.

I've always had a lot of male friends and seem to get on better with men than with certain women: especially the silly, frilly types who are obsessed with makeup, hair and housework. I suppose I relate more to butch women. When I was little I hated dolls and used to cut their hair off. I much preferred playing with my brother's Scalextrix and sword fighting. Later, I was into cars and finding out how they worked. Ray and I used to go to customised car shows together.

I liked being 'one of the boys' and going around in jeans, pumps and one of my dad's old baggy jumpers with a wide belt. I think Mum always wanted me to be the Pretty Girl with long flowing blonde hair in ribbons and frilly dresses. I've never been like that. I've always been a jeans and T-shirt person. I like to wear clothes I feel comfortable in and that express me as a person. Sometimes, when I went home at weekends from boarding school, I would find that Mum had been out shopping and bought me some dresses. 'I can't possibly wear that!' I'd say. So, in the end, it was decided that she would give me my own money to go and buy clothes.

One of the things that Ray found difficult was that I am not the type of girl who would spend hours in front of the mirror painting her face and fiddling with her hair. He would sometimes say to me: 'Why don't you put on a dress today?' 'No way,' I'd say. If people don't like me the way I am, that's just tough. I have never let a man tell me what to do, and I never will.

We both liked cars, CB, exploring different places in a group, but I was very career minded and Ray wasn't, and that was what finally drove us apart. I wanted to go forwards, while he was content to settle down and stay put.

It was a period when I was becoming very liberated in my ideas. I think it all started when I saw the way my mum was expected to do everything in the house, and I knew that whoever I settled down with would have to pull his weight because I wanted more from life than hoovering, dusting and cleaning toilets.

I'd been influenced a great deal by my work with young people, and by my colleagues: men who were kind, considerate and non-sexist, men who believed in sharing and knew where they were at. All this was a revelation to me and helped to radicalise my thinking.

About six months after my name had gone on the housing list I happened to be staying with Jackie Fletcher in Wakefield and my mum rang me there to say the council had been trying to track me down. They wanted me to go and see the site of my new flat at Rickmansworth. I returned home immediately and went round to see it. They were building a block of six flats, one for a disabled person. At this stage it was just a hole in the ground, but I was excited at the prospect of one day having a place of my own.

I moved into my new ground-floor purpose-built flat in September 1982, after an eighteen-month wait. It was designed with special modifications: ramps up to the doors, no steps, hand rails, lever taps, power points halfway up the walls.

I started out with the most diabolical furniture, most of it acquired through the Classifieds in our local paper: an old carpet, an assortment of pots and pans, an enormous ancient black and white telly that probably fell off a lorry . . . Third-hand stuff, but it served me well.

My CB friends helped me move in and laid my carpet for me. We all had quite a few laughs in the process, and for about the first six months it was a bit like living in a commune.

It took me a while to adjust to coming home to my own place and having to do my own washing, shopping and cooking . . . but it was freedom and it was all mine.

Ray was a good handyman, but when it came to household chores, he was reluctant to do his share. He used to come over in the evening and expect a meal to be waiting. I told him he was just as capable of cooking a meal as I was. He didn't like that. There was friction between us and I began to realise: 'This is a no-no relationship.'

There were old people in the block. It's funny how the disabled and the old always seem to get lumped together! When we had parties we tried to keep the noise down, but they must have heard some of it.

The main drawback was being without a telephone for a year, though I was able to use my neighbour's. It was great having my own *space* and organising it exactly as I wished.

Around the time that I moved into the flat, my brother was having a bad time at home. One of my mum's favourite sayings is: 'You're using this house like a hotel.' I'd had this said to *me* a few times, and now it was Andy's turn! After a row at home, he would ask me if he could come and stay at the flat for the odd night. I agreed — and that changed everything. It meant that our earlier roles were reversed and instead of Andrew being protective of *me*, I was the one looking after *him*, because he was staying in *my* home on *my* terms. It shifted the balance of power in our relationship and made Andy see me in quite a different light.

When he was only about ten years old I can remember him saying to me: 'When Mum and Dad die you will have to come and live with me so that I can look after you.' I was very angry at the time and told him not to be so stupid. Even then, I was determined to have my own place. But there was always the assumption among family and friends that I would never be independent and that Andy would be left to take care of me. This was taken for granted. It was almost as if Mum and Dad had made him think of it in those terms — as a kind of duty. Nobody in the world thought I would ever marry or lead an independent life. Not even my closest friends believed that I would succeed in holding down a job *and* run my own flat — but I did! I think that is what makes me want to try so many things on my own — because the prevailing view was: Poor Alison, Andrew will have to look after her one day.

I needed to have my own space, car, job, just like anybody else. Before taking on the flat, my dad said to me: 'Alison, if you want to come home don't hesitate.' It's interesting that he hardly ever came to see me there. He'd been the boss at home for so long that I think he felt uneasy with me in charge in my own place.

My mum, although she worried about me, was able to disguise her feelings more effectively than Dad. She came to visit once a week, and I still went to see them quite often.

Knowing that nobody believed I would cope on my own

made me all the more determined to prove them wrong. The idea that disabled people are low achievers has been reinforced to such an extent that it is often self-perpetuating. Because other people's expectations are so low, when one does achieve something of importance everyone goes wild!

It was like when I was invited to Buckingham Palace to meet the Queen. This came about in 1983 through my involvement in The Pack and was in the form of a reception to mark the twenty-first Anniversary of Community Service Volunteers. I was sent a formal invitation.

The Master of the Household
has received Her Majesty's command
to invite
Miss Alison French
to a Reception to be given at Buckingham Palace
by the Queen and the Duke of Edinburgh

(Day dress. No hats.)

My friend Karen came with me. I didn't want Ray to tag along, and it's a bit naff taking your mum to Buckingham Palace, so I asked Karen instead. She worked with me in the same office at youth and community. We did projects together, and she became a good mate of mine. She was freaky and punky, with red streaked spiky hair.

We both tarted ourselves up for the occasion. I wore a smart blue and white striped day dress, white shoes and more makeup than usual. We arrived at 6.0 p.m. for cocktails in the Green Room, and later I moved into the Ballroom, where I met the Queen. There were butlers in white gloves and wigs, tied with ribbons at the back. We had sandwiches without the crusts: cucumber and cheese, and fishpaste — the kind that disappear in one mouthful. I was more impressed with the way the footman kept our glasses topped up with wine, and by the end of the evening I was feeling quite happy.

Half the attraction of going to the Palace was receiving the official invitation through the post from the Queen. I felt very honoured.

7

Meeting Mark

Early in 1984 I began my basic part-time training for youth and community work: this was a condition of my appointment with SW Herts. I had to go to the youth service building in Carey Place for one evening a week for twenty weeks, starting and ending with a residential weekend at All Saints Pastoral Centre, a retreat house at London Colney, near St Albans.

I was rather halfhearted about doing this course as I had already applied to study for a professional certificate in youth and community work in Walthamstow, North London. About forty people from across the county came to London Colney on the Friday evening of the first residential weekend, and as far as I can remember, I was the only physically disabled person there. We divided into different groups and I was with Karen, Diane and Cynthia, all co-workers from my area.

We spent most of the weekend performing various tasks, and the final task involved each of us approaching somebody whom we didn't know and telling them what we had noticed or picked up about them at the weekend. Since our arrival Karen and I had been eyeing up the local talent: the best looking blokes, the ones who seemed worth getting to know

— and we both decided, from our own personal observations, that Mark John came out on top.

So, for this particular task, Karen dared me to go up and speak to him. A dare, to me, is irresistible, so I went up to this tall, dark, well-built man, pinned him in a corner and announced: 'My name is Alison. I think you are Welsh, you drink beer a lot and you play rugby.' He was almost dumbstruck. He was standing against the wall in a very laid-back, open posture. Suddenly, his face went blank and I could sense that he felt embarrassed by the fact that somebody had put him 'on the spot' and that the somebody in question happened to be physically disabled.

It was the first time I had actually spoken to him, but he said nothing in reply except a tentative: 'Yes.' I thought: 'What a wally!' I was not impressed.

After the weekend we all went back to our respective areas (Mark was based in St Albans) and in the intervening weeks I had virtually forgotten all about him. To me, he was just a bloke I'd met who was reasonably good-looking.

When we returned to London Colney for the follow-up weekend, in June, all the groups were split up so that this time we were working with people we didn't know, from other areas. And guess who was in my group? — Mark John!

My initial reaction on walking into the room and seeing him there was: 'Oh *no*!' He sat sprawled out in his combat trousers and green T-shirt, and he was puffing away on his pipe (this put me off as I dislike anything that smokes). He seemed embarrassed to see me again, especially as this time we were both involved in the same group.

There were about eight of us in the group, and nobody knew quite what to do to set the ball rolling, so I said: 'Let's introduce ourselves. Hello, my name is Alison' — and so on, with each person saying a few words about themselves. It was a get-to-know-you routine, a way of testing the 'dynamics' of the new group.

We all got on very well. In fact, we managed to upset a few tutors by laughing too loudly and so, in a way, we defeated the main object, which was to see how we worked together under pressure: there *was* no pressure, because we all 'gelled' so well.

On the Saturday afternoon we were all lying in the grass in the sun outside, talking about what we were going to do with our lives, and Mark said he was training to be a priest. At first I really believed he was pulling my leg. This extrovert man with the infectious laugh just didn't square with my own mental picture of what a 'real' priest would be like. With my anti-religious sentiments, I thought: 'He's not for me,' and decided to keep my distance.

As part of its presentation, each group had to complete a short project. We felt that our group had been misjudged and misunderstood by the other groups, who had perceived us as being flippant and uncaring, and to redress the balance we set out to make a video which would show us in a more serious light. We chose as our theme a mock riot scene, which could be interpreted in one of a number of ways.

We staged a scene where one person was throwing a bomb or other missile at somebody else. We had three news presenters reading the news and showed how all three read that particular item in a different way and so gave a different picture, which is what we felt had happened to *us*. Other people had 'read' our group wrongly.

After the day's training was over we began working on our project and continued until quite late that evening. At about nine o'clock we had a break. We all decided to go to the bar and buy in plenty of booze before closing time so that we could drink into the night while we were working. I remember it so clearly — Mark was standing on my left at the bar and he asked me if I'd like a drink. 'OK, I'll have half a lager,' I said and took my straws out of my bag. He looked at me rather quizzically.

'I always drink through a straw because you get pissed quicker that way,' I said. This broke the ice completely, and we immediately hit it off and had a whale of a time.

Having brought a large supply of lager back to the seminar room, we all stayed up until about 3.0 a.m. drinking and working on our project. We got pretty drunk and things were being said that would otherwise perhaps have been left unsaid. We were having deep, meaningful discussions about emotions and how we felt about life. It wasn't, 'My mum works in Sainsbury's.' Mark told me he liked me, but I didn't take him seriously. In any case, I wasn't looking for another bloke. After all, I still had steady, sensible, above-board Ray to come back to. Both Mark and I were treading warily. Mark was still working on his own deepseated hangups about disability in general (and mine in particular), while *I* continued to have grave doubts about his priestly aspirations.

The following day (Sunday), heavily hung over, we presented our finished project to the other groups. Their response was favourable and we felt we had redeemed ourselves as a result.

Then it came to saying goodbye. We all got together for a cup of tea, and because we were such a close-knit group there were lots of kisses and cuddles. I went around kissing everybody, and when I reached Mark he kissed me on the forehead. I was a bit taken aback by this. With the others, it had been cheeks or lips. 'OK. Fair enough. If that's how you want it,' I thought.

I drove home to my flat and back to Ray, who was not in the least interested in hearing about my weekend and could relate to none of it.

Several days passed. I was fully occupied at work, in and around Watford. Then, one day Karen and I were sent over to Mark's area on a project. Karen phoned Dee Hamilton, Mark's youth leader in St Albans, to organise a meeting with her at the youth and community centre there. Unknown to me, Karen had asked her to arrange for Mark to be there when I arrived.

We drove to St Albans in my car and there at the centre to meet us was Mark. This time I actually got a hug, so *something* must have registered in his head since our previous meeting. As for me, I was still unaware of any deep feelings for him at this stage.

After we had talked for a while to Dee Hamilton, Mark invited Karen and me back for lunch at his flat in the city centre, which he shared with a trainee Methodist minister. Karen and I nearly died when we saw the place. It was like walking into a pigsty. The toilet window was broken, the bathroom sink was blocked and hanging off the wall, propped up with a chair. It was disgusting.

There was no food anywhere in the flat and he had to go out and buy some, which shows how much he was trying to impress me!

We sat at the kitchen table eating eggs, chips, sausages and beans. Mark was opposite me, Karen to my right, and we were chatting about our home lives. For some reason Ray's name came up in the conversation. Mark didn't know that I already had a boyfriend and apparently (I don't remember this, but Karen told me later) his face fell . . .

We decided that it might be a nice idea to organise a reunion for everyone on the course, and Mark suggested having a disco in the crypt of St Albans Abbey, so Karen and I rounded up the Watford crowd and Mark took charge of the St Albans and Hertford faction.

A date for the disco was fixed for about a month ahead, on

a Friday evening. I gave Karen a lift in my car and we arrived at the crypt to be greeted by Mark in shirt, tie and suit. He looked quite respectable and went up in my estimation.

We went first to the Fighting Cocks, the oldest pub in England, and got pretty happy, then back to the crypt for the disco. About thirty of us turned up, including some tutors. Karen and I were dancing away, while Mark had a drink with his cronies. Everyone was having a good time, and the atmosphere felt relaxed and happy.

Early on in the evening, it was mainly reggae music. Later, when the slow records started, Mark came over towards me and he didn't *ask* me to dance: he grabbed me by the arm and dragged me on to the floor. Lionel Ritchie's 'Hello' was playing at the time. We were dancing quite closely and I had my arms around his neck, he had his arms around my waist. I remember thinking how nice his eyes were. There was no kissing or anything. We were just *close*.

Karen was behind Mark, dancing with another bloke and giving me the wink and the old thumbs-up across the floor.

Having that physical contact with Mark certainly made me reconsider my feelings about our relationship. He was definitely on my wavelength: I knew that from the course. We'd been thrown together for two weekends in very highly charged, intense circumstances and each of us had learned how the other one worked. What we had yet to find out were the more basic details — the ordinary social exchanges or platitudes of couples on first meeting, like: 'Where are you from?' 'Have you brothers and sisters?' So, in a curious way, our relationship was moving in reverse from a deeper level to a more down-to-earth one.

After dancing to Lionel Ritchie we sat talking for a while until the party broke up around 1.0 a.m. It came to a rather abrupt halt after the Dean of St Albans, who lived nearby, had a quiet word with Mark about the noise we were making.

People started drifting off home. Mark issued an open invitation to coffee at his flat, which was about a mile away. Most of us were too sloshed to drive, but one way or another we arrived at the flat, where cups of hot, strong coffee were handed around. We turned the music up, danced and talked about what a wonderful world we lived in and how we would change it singlehandedly.

Then, somehow I found myself in Mark's bedroom. We just sat on the king-size bed talking. People kept banging on the door and wanting to come in — including Karen, who said to me: 'Come on, Alison, we'd better be going.'

I went to the loo and left her talking to Mark. When I came out she whispered to me: 'You can't go home, Alison — he doesn't want you to.' I went back into the bedroom and Mark said: 'Please stay and talk to me.' Well, I just melted there and then . . .

Karen managed to get a lift home with somebody else. Meanwhile, about half a dozen of us stayed up most of the night talking. We eventually fell asleep, all of us piled on top of the bed.

I woke up at about eight o'clock on Saturday morning, surrounded by all these bodies and my first thought was: 'Bloody hell, how did I get here? What did I do last night?' I knew I couldn't have done anything much as I was still fully dressed, so that was OK . . . but I felt lousy. Other people around me were waking up groaning about their sore heads.

Then I remembered Ray. I was supposed to be seeing him that morning and I was bound to be late back.

Mark asked me if I could run him into work before heading for home. He was working part-time in the Fighting Cocks to finance his year's youth work in the parish. I drove him there and before he got out of the car he asked if he could see me again. I suggested that he ring me at work (I had no phone in the flat then), and we left it like that.

I knew I would be in big trouble with Ray, as I was still wearing all my party gear, and by the time I reached my flat he was waiting outside in his car for me, demanding to know where I'd been.

'Shopping!' I said.

'Oh no you haven't.'

'Oh yes I have.'

'You've been with that Mark, haven't you?'

I couldn't give a damn any more and we had a blazing row. We went out on his boat on the river for the weekend, but it was a disaster. We simply weren't communicating. Whenever Ray spoke, which wasn't often, Mark's name was attached to nearly every sentence. I found it equally hard to keep Mark's name out of our limited conversation, and I spent most of the time in a daydream.

I went to work as usual on the Monday and didn't see Ray for the next few weeks, mainly because I was working quite hard but also because I'd had more than enough of his pettiness.

About a fortnight after the party, Karen and I happened to be over in St Albans and I said: 'Let's go and find Mark.' We drove to the Abbey, where we found him with some friends from the course from my area. One of them, Jim, had an open Land Rover and we all piled in and went to the Fighting Cocks, then back to Mark's flat for a coffee before returning to Watford.

Mark walked me to the car and for the first time we had a proper snog together. Karen sat in the car with her hand on the horn to hurry me up as it was getting late and we were supposed to be back at work.

I got in the car, feeling totally confused, and said: 'Tell me this is not happening, Karen.'

Later, Karen came over to my flat and we talked for hours. She's a good friend but her advice wasn't particularly helpful.

It was along the lines of: 'It's time you sorted yourself out.' I was left on the horns of an emotional dilemma. On the one hand, there was this priestly person who was great fun and shared my sense of humour, and on the other hand, there was this steady but rather boring guy who was giving me a hard time. I knew in my heart that my relationship with Ray was on the wane and that it was only a matter of time before the final goodbye.

Mark and I saw each other for a couple of weeks on and off; then, at the beginning of August (1984) he went on holiday to France for three weeks with his friend Duncan and Duncan's girlfriend. This had been arranged some time before, but it left me in a deep state of flux.

8

Beating the Church Barrier

After Mark had gone to France, Ray and I had one almighty showdown. I said to him: 'We can't go on like this any longer.' He kept saying: 'Yes, I know . . . but I still love you.' I told him my feelings for him had changed and there was no going back.

Ray was the type who wanted to protect me, whereas Mark just wanted to *support* me. When Ray left, I thought: 'Good. Now I can get on with my life.' Being dumped by somebody disabled must be pretty shattering and his ego must have taken quite a dent.

Meanwhile, I became more and more involved with my work and was very busy within the community, visiting youth clubs and PHAB clubs. Karen and I were also helping to organise an exhibition in Hertford promoting the county's youth service, taking turns to man a stall there. This went on for three weeks.

One morning I received a letter from Mark in which he wrote: 'Having a good time. Thinking a lot about you and me, and would like us to continue . . . PS I love you.'

My immediate reaction was: 'How can he love me? He doesn't know me well enough.' I was becoming fonder of him by the minute and we enjoyed each other's company, but as far as I was concerned, it was a question of liking rather than love. We were able to talk freely about almost anything, and I guess the 'falling in love' bit developed from that.

Duncan was Mark's best friend and while they were away in France, Mark said to Duncan: 'I think I'm falling in love with a spastic.' Apparently, Duncan was very hostile and said: 'Don't do it.' I gather that for the entire three weeks he and his girlfriend had to put up with Mark talking about me and saying how much he was missing me.

When they got back Mark arranged for me to meet Duncan. I had to pass the 'acid test': if Duncan liked and accepted me, then everything was fine.

We went out for dinner at a Berni Inn. Mark was so anxious for Duncan to like me that to prepare him for our encounter he must have built me up to be some kind of monster or dragon so that the reality would be less awful. He was still working on his own inhibitions about my disability and was worried about what his friends might think.

I don't quite know what Duncan was expecting, but we established an instant rapport. I think he was pleasantly shocked by my sense of humour. I am quick at banter and picking up jokes. I am not slow 'upstairs', as they say. Duncan may have anticipated a more placid, phlegmatic type of person, but then Mark would never have fallen in love with anybody like that. Being a big, rather loud, hyperactive kind of bloke, Mark needed somebody with a strong personality to cope with that, otherwise he could walk all over you.

Mark has one other very close friend, Simon Fricker, to whom he had painted a similarly unflattering picture of me, but again, Simon and I hit it off right from the start.

My twenty-first birthday was approaching and some of our friends came round to celebrate: Tim and other CB friends, work colleagues, Mark and Mark's brother Simon. We walked to the local pub, the Feathers, which was about a quarter of a mile from my flat.

Unknown to me, Simon was spiking my drinks. Consequently, not only was I drinking Martini but a mixture of gin, lager and vodka too. As the drinks were piling up, I was getting very happy. When it was time for Last Orders, I went to get up to buy a round and found that I couldn't move. I was absolutely legless, and when I'm like that I become very floppy and very giggly.

When we finally got home somebody suggested that we had something to eat (we'd had no food all evening). My friend Tim drove to the Chinese takeaway and came back with four or five carrier bags containing various dishes, chucked them on the table and everyone helped themselves. I promptly threw up, and I felt quite poorly afterwards.

Some people stayed the night. I just went to bed and left them to it. I remember Mark waking me up with a cup of tea at about 10.0 a.m. I felt awful. He said: 'Listen, I've got something to tell you.' I thought maybe the car had been knocked, but it was nothing like that . . .

'You kissed a policeman last night,' said Mark. I was horrified. I couldn't remember anything about the latter part of the evening. He told me I'd gone up to this policeman and started chatting him up and kissing him and that the officer wanted to see me about it. Everyone teased me about this for ages and I believed them at first, they fooled me completely.

Later on that day we all felt hungry, so we sent out for fish and chips and more booze. We got plastered all over again, and the partying went on for the whole weekend.

I don't need a straw when I'm drunk, because I feel so relaxed. All the tension disappears from my body, and I stop wobbling. I sway a bit, but I don't wobble as I normally do. If you saw me when I was drunk you wouldn't think I was disabled at all. But I don't like being in that state because it means I'm not in control of my body. I won't ever get drunk if Mark is not around.

Pimms is my favourite drink, but I mostly drink lager as then I can stay sober longer. If I don't feel happy in a situation then I'll drink to give myself Dutch courage.

I recovered in time to enjoy my birthday dinner at the Old Barn restaurant in St Albans. My parents had arranged to take me there and I asked them if I could invite Mark. 'What about Ray?' they said, and when I told them our relationship was over they seemed relieved as they had believed all along he would be wrong for me.

It was the first time Mark had met my parents. My dad was his usual outspoken self and deeply suspicious of Mark's religious inclinations. 'Don't come here preaching to us. We won't have any of your religion here,' he said. I think he reckoned I was off with some mad bible basher, but Mark didn't pay too much attention to this and they all ended up on amicable terms. (In fact, afterwards, both my parents started going to church again, not that Mark claims any credit for this.)

Andy wasn't there: he's never been very family-oriented. It was a dinner dance and Mark and I danced together between courses and after the meal. We got on so well and it seemed like we had known each other for years and years.

Meanwhile, Ray was trying to get back on the scene. One Friday evening after work Mark came over to my flat. Both of us being sports fans, we stayed up to watch the Olympics. Then I went to bed and Mark curled up on the settee in the lounge.

The following morning Ray phoned and asked if he could come round and see me. I told him Mark was there and what he said then wasn't very nice. I suggested it might be a good idea if he came over and met Mark. I felt the only way of getting the message across to him was to be open and upfront about the situation.

When he arrived I kept out of the way while words were said between him and Mark. The visit was brief and Ray was coldly polite to both of us. I told him: 'I want you to leave now and please don't come back.' He went off in a huff.

But it was not quite the end of the story. A couple of months later Mark discovered the words 'Holy Bastard' sprayed in large white letters across the boot of his car. As soon as he told me this I went storming up to Ray's house and blew my top. Ray denied over and over again that he was the culprit, but I knew of nobody else who would be likely to have done such a thing.

When Mark telephoned his parents in Builth Wells and told them he was bringing me home to meet them, Mark's mother asked if there was anything I needed. 'Just straws,' he said.

The first thing she did when we arrived was to grab me to help me walk. 'Don't worry. I can manage,' I told her, and went to the loo to calm myself down. I was terribly nervous about meeting his parents. His father is a clergyman (a canon of Brecon Cathedral), his mother an art teacher.

He has three brothers: Paul, Simon, Philip. Simon and I are quite close. I think I helped him find his direction in life: he is now working with mentally handicapped people in London.

We spent about a week with his parents and it went off quite well, though they were both shocked when they saw us holding hands and kissing. Apparently, neither of them had realised that we were more than just *friends* — and yet Mark had brought other girlfriends home before me and his parents had never assumed *they* were platonic!

I think I understand what they were really 'saying': they were concerned that I might cling too much, cramp his style, prevent him advancing in his career. How independent was I? How much time would he need to put aside to look after me?

In the early stages of our relationship Mark wanted to do *everything* for me, which used to get on my nerves. We had a blazing row about it and I told him: 'If you don't learn to leave me alone, you can go.' I think it showed up *his* inadequacies as well — the fact that he wasn't able to sit back and recognise that it takes me just a bit longer to do certain things but I'll get there in the end.

I remember once when he asked me round for dinner at his flat in St Albans. His flatmate, the trainee Methodist minister, David, was there as well. The three of us sat down to dinner and I asked Mark if he would cut up my meat for me. He cut the meat into tiny, baby-like pieces. I just looked at him — and my plate — and said: 'My mouth is as big as yours, you know.' Poor Mark went bright red, and even his normally studious, serious flatmate started laughing . . .

In September 1984 Mark began his three-year training for the priesthood at St Stephen's House, Oxford. We saw each other alternate weekends. Oxford is about an hour's drive from Rickmansworth and I drove there one weekend, he visited me the next. In term time we rang each other almost every day.

It was my first weekend to visit Mark. I had no idea quite what to expect. As I saw it, St Stephen's House was a college for training vicars and I had formed a picture in my mind of a quiet, old-fashioned, churchy place with dark rooms and rules of silence.

I drove to Oxford on the Friday and headed in the direction of the college, which was a tall, old house in beautiful grounds in Manston Street, just off the main Cowley Road. I struggled up a flight of about ten steep stone steps to the front door, rang the bell and waited. Somebody — a fellow student, I think — came and ushered me into the main reception area and then went off to find Mark.

It was about 4.0 p.m. . . . I was petrified, full of nervous anticipation. Mark appeared and took me into the lounge, where tea was being served. It was a long room with high ceilings. Small groups of men were gathered in corners, drinking tea and talking earnestly in loud whispers. It was a bit like being in a library.

We had tea and biscuits brought to us on a trolley. If I hadn't felt so nervous I'd probably have laughed. I could feel laughter bubbling up inside me.

I felt most uncomfortable, not because I was the only female in a room full of men but because I had no way of knowing what was (or was not) regarded as acceptable behaviour. Could one talk? — or swear? I was unusually silent, unsure of my role.

Mark introduced me as his girlfriend and I met a lot of really nice people. Unfortunately, he had to go to a tutorial and was away for well over an hour, leaving me there surrounded by all these men.

Later I joined Mark for the evening meal in the large dining hall. Before we sat down we had to say Grace, but I hadn't realised this and was already in my seat while everyone else was standing. I felt so embarrassed at this *faux pas* of mine, but Mark put me at my ease.

Fish was on the menu, and the religious bit in me made a mental note: 'Fish on Friday. I must remember that if Mark comes and stays.'

The college Principal and tutors were seated at the top table and there were several rows of tables down the sides of the room, where the students sat. I remember being conscious that I was one of the very few women present.

After the meal was over several of us went out to the Red, White and Blue pub, which is across the road from the college. Things changed completely then. These young student priests were dressed more casually, and they were drinking, smoking cigars and telling rude jokes — just like any other group of men. This came as quite a shock to me after the sedate atmosphere of the tea lounge.

I can honestly say that it was the first time I have been in a new situation where so many people went out of their way to speak to me and make me feel so at home. Like Mark, most of them called me Ally or Al, and I almost became part of the life of the college. Whenever there were any big events or parties I'd always be invited, and when I rang Mark his friends would enquire about me and send their love.

Mark was one of a new intake of about a dozen students. It was hard work maintaining our relationship because, although I knew Mark pretty well by this time, he was going through a process of great personal change and I needed to allow for this.

He was becoming more set in his views on certain issues, like the ordination of women (he is anti, I am pro, a source of continuing debate between us), and his superiors were constantly testing out his vocation. *I*, too, felt obliged to challenge him in my own non-religious way.

Mark has always stipulated that I should simply keep an open mind about religion, and that is what I try to do. What sustains me is inquisitiveness. I will always endeavour to understand, and to ask questions — and that is good for Mark's faith as well.

We discuss questions like: 'How do we know that God exists?' 'How can Mary be a virgin?' — the kinds of issues which I find almost impossible to comprehend, and which I will throw back to Mark for clarification.

I'll say: 'How can God be a loving god if there are so many

people in the world with serious disabilities?' Mark says he can't answer that one and tells me: 'Your faith will carry you through,' but I think that is my greatest difficulty. I am a person who likes to see results and to have full knowledge of what is happening. Otherwise, my doubts remain. The more I hear and learn about religion, the more it makes me think, and I still find it all very confusing. I definitely believe there must be another level of consciousness apart from this world because, if there isn't, then some of us have had a pretty bad deal.

Mark and I were committed to each other within the first three months of our relationship. I felt I had found my soulmate, my life partner, and I know he felt the same about me. We declared our love for each other and expressed it in an intimate way.

We both needed to have physical contact with one another, especially Mark who needed to get over his fears and hangups about touching somebody who had a disability. Although in theory he had accepted my disability, it's different when it comes to sleeping with somebody and making love.

There is also the point which arouses many people's curiosity: 'Can they actually *do* it?' Disabled people are considered to be incapable of enjoying a satisfactory sex life. We aren't supposed to have sexual feelings . . . Like any other woman, I was nervous about my first full sexual relationship. 'What will it be like?' 'Does it hurt?' But I had no qualms in relation to my disability. I knew I could kiss and cuddle. I knew I had all the right bits in the right places, and there were no problems on that score.

Living in an establishment of sixty or so men and a handful of women (cooks, cleaners and one nun), Mark was confronted for the first time with male homosexuality. In the accommodation block there were landings with rooms leading off. Mark felt that he was one of the only 'straight' (heterosexual) men on his landing, and at the beginning he found that a bit intimidating. I told him he would have to learn to come to terms with this, and he did. We both did. In fact, as our relationship developed, we became very close to the gay men at St Stephen's House. Extra-marital relationships of any kind were frowned upon by the Church, and we could identify with the gay community in their need for discretion.

It made me feel uneasy that in the Church's eyes my relationship with Mark was acceptable but to be homosexual was to be condemned to a life of secrecy and prejudice and to be denied the same rights and freedoms automatically given to heterosexuals. Both Mark and I felt unhappy about these double standards.

There were a lot of hidden agendas. Some of the gay men at St Stephen's House had been very repressed but were slowly beginning to come out of the closet, and I wanted to support them in doing that. It's hard for all gay people to say: 'I am what I am,' especially in the current climate of fear and hostility generated by the AIDS scare.

For Mark and me, the biggest barrier was still the religious one. If the person you love believes in something that is beyond your understanding, it cuts you off and alienates you from each other. In a way, I felt jealous of Mark's faith, though we did go to church together on Sunday mornings. It was part of a deal we made between us, a condition of our relationship: that I would try to overcome my scepticism and acquire my own faith and convictions by regular churchgoing. St Stephen's House have their own church, attached to the college. I had always been frightened off going to church as I equated it with behaving myself, dressing up and wearing hats. That was my own stereotyped image of Christian worship.

Mark's mother warned me that the Church would become his mistress. She may have been trying to put me off marrying him. I think she found it difficult accepting that her son could love a physically disabled woman, but her remarks had no effect on me at all — except perhaps to reinforce my feelings for Mark.

It was quite clear by this time that it would be Mark and Alison forever. We trusted one another implicitly, and we were each mature enough to go off to separate colleges for two or three years, get qualified and come together afterwards. In any case, I didn't fall in love with a priest: I fell in love with a person called Mark.

9

'If you want to take the piss, do it in front of me'

In September 1985 Mark had completed one year at St Stephen's House when I began my two-year course in youth and community work at the YMCA National College in Walthamstow, North London. This came about at the suggestion of my boss, Mike Hockings. Mike said to me: 'Look, Alison, if you want to continue in this kind of work, you need a professional qualification.' I hesitated. It would be a big step for me to take. After all, I'd had no standard education, no O or A level certificates to show for my years of schooling. Further study was a daunting prospect and I honestly believed I was too thick even to get on to a course, let alone finish it and qualify. I needed loads of support from Mike, Mark and my parents. They all said: 'Go for it, Alison.'

I must be the only applicant there ever to have had two interviews. Two weeks before the main interview, they gave me an extra grilling. A letter had arrived inviting me to go for an interview, and I was really excited about this. When I got there, the tutor did nothing except talk about my disability and how I would cope with the workload and so on. At the time I thought this was a bit strange for a formal interview.

After about an hour he said he would write and tell me when my *interview* was. So I said to him: 'Well, what was *this*?' He explained that it was 'just a chat to enable us to get to know each other'. I said: 'Do you do that with *all* prospective students?' 'No,' he said. I felt deflated. I'd worked myself up for nothing.

A couple of weeks later I went for the interview proper, which lasted all day. They asked me questions like: 'What would you do if a gang were fighting in your youth club?' I also had to submit in advance a piece of writing about two thousand words in length. Subject: 'How do you see yourself as a youth worker?' I had already gained some useful experience in youth work and I think they could see that I had potential and wanted very much to do the course. So they accepted me and SW Herts awarded me a full student grant.

There was a good mix of students in my year, evenly balanced between men and women, black and white, though I was the only disabled student.

In my first year I lived in the YMCA hostel alongside the college. Six of us shared most of the top floor, including Karen II (Karen I was my friend from youth and community), David and Joan. I had my own room and there was a communal bathroom and kitchen.

For the first couple of weeks people went to bed on time and everything was very respectable, but gradually, as we got to know each other better, our social life became quite hectic. Our tiny kitchen became a popular meeting place where we used to get together and drink cups of coffee. Sometimes we were joined by other students from our year.

My room was right opposite the kitchen, and so it was always *my* radio and cassette player that was on and people would wander in and out changing tapes.

We all mucked in together with shopping and cooking. I

was the only one with a car and on Mondays everyone used to pile in to go shopping at Sainsbury's in Walthamstow.

Karen, who was around thirty, wanted to become a vegetarian and we experimented with lots of dishes like vegetable lasagne, with different sauces. We had some good fun doing that.

David was Irish, with a strong accent which it took me quite a while to understand properly. He was a lovely person and always had a store of Irish jokes to share.

We went out in the evenings a fair bit, first to the local pub down the road. Later on, when we became more adventurous, we would drive into London, to the East End. We explored the yuppie areas to find the wine bars.

In December Karen and I went into the West End to do our Christmas shopping. I remember taking the day off college to go to Harrods. Neither of us had been there before, and we walked around the store open-mouthed. Everything you see on display there is so expensive and so beautifully presented. We just ended up having a cup of coffee without buying anything.

What I found interesting was that about half the people who were on my college course were from some kind of religious background. It was very stimulating to be surrounded by all these different beliefs. David was a Protestant, my church is more 'high church' (Anglo-Catholic), and Karen was from one of the newer, evangelical-style denominations, so she would put in her pennyworth as well. We had some fiery debates about which aspects of each were right, which were wrong, but we always ended up good friends.

As always, the first term was the worst. My peers in my year were brilliant, writing down my notes for me and helping to type my essays. I can read a chapter in an hour or so, but actually writing down what I wanted to say would take me ages, and I was under a lot of stress. I was lucky as my tutors did allow me to hand in most of my essays on tape, which was helpful.

The course was based on a system of continuous assessment and consisted of a combination of tutorials, seminars and lectures. I wondered what the hell I'd got myself into. I was missing Mark terribly. I used to phone him in tears and beg him to come and fetch me. Tutors used words like 'interaction', 'ego', and so on. It was like another language and at first I couldn't understand a word. After years of living in an academic wilderness I suddenly found myself writing essays on psychology, or Marxist theory.

My personal tutor was Peter Harding, who was wonderfully supportive and gave me time to look at myself, where I was at and where I needed to go in the future. He took a genuine interest in me and I really appreciated my hour a week with him. Some students would groan and say: 'Oh *no* . . . Got a tutorial. What an earth will I talk about?' But *I* couldn't wait to get in there and see Peter!

There was a good rapport between us. We didn't just talk about college work. We talked about my childhood, about what it meant to be disabled. I was able to explore my feelings about different areas of my life, and I owe him a lot for that. It was an hour when I was able to bounce ideas off Peter and know that he would listen. He usually turned around my questions and made me answer them myself.

I missed those sessions for quite a long time afterwards. They could be very emotional. Some of the things I didn't understand about myself when I first went to college — like why I felt angry and frustrated — became clearer to me by the end.

Sometimes I would go in and see Peter and tell him: 'I've had enough. I'm leaving.'

'Why do you want to leave, Alison?' he'd say, very calm. I didn't really want to give up the course: it was just my sense of frustration at not always being able to keep pace with the others. He made me think twice about it, look rationally at the situation.

I used to compensate for my learning difficulties by staying up late to catch up on my reading. My fellow students and I would often discuss and argue well into the night — about lectures we'd attended during the day and about our studies generally.

How I changed in those two years! I went through hell with myself. I began to realise I had been cheated on for most of my life and made to feel worthless, second class. I'd been seen and treated as a low achiever. What society wants and requires is recognised paper qualifications, an asset which had so far been denied me (apart from some English Speaking Board papers and City and Guilds cookery exams, none of which have much 'clout').

I'd missed out in so many ways in my growing-up. Missed the ordinary experiences enjoyed by able-bodied young people: the basic skills of making and meeting friends, going to discos, having a variety of boyfriends . . . My life had been far too sheltered.

Then I met Joan, who broadened my perspective a lot and became a close friend. Joan is a lesbian. She had a hangup at first about being gay. One night, not long after the beginning of term, we were talking and she said: 'Alison, I've got a disability.'

'What do you mean?' I asked her.

'I'm gay,' she said.

'OK,' I replied. I didn't think: 'How disgusting.' Joan must have known that I wouldn't be shocked. She knew that some of Mark's gay fellow-students had been to see me at college and she'd met them.

I said to her: 'Why try to pretend to be something you're not? I mean, for goodness' sake, *I* can't hide what I am, so why hide what *you* are?'

Although Joan had relationships with other girls at college, it took her most of the two years to come to terms with being a lesbian. I was the first 'straight' person she told at college and this brought us very close.

Straight . . . gay . . . They are just more labels. I believe that everyone goes through a close, same-sex relationship phase, not necessarily sexual. In my own case, it was with Jenny (at Lonsdale). Sometimes we shared the same bed, we stayed in each other's houses and confided in one another.

Joan took me to my very first gay night club, the Black Cap in Camden Town, North London, and it was a good experience for me. The place was packed and everyone seemed to be paired off. I was tagging along with Joan and people must have thought I was a spare part! There I was, trying to be cool and sophisticated, but mixing with gay people *en masse* came as a bit of a shock to me.

Joan used to go and tell her friends to ask me to dance, and when I went to the toilet someone asked if I'd like a hand. Joan cracked up laughing when I told her!

During my first year, I saw my parents about once a week, for Friday dinners. My father had been keen for me to do the course but worried about my physically being able to keep pace with the other students and, intellectually, coping with lectures and so on. He felt at first that I may have bitten off more than I could chew.

The college workload was heavy, but my mind had been starved for so long that I just wanted more and more mental stimulation.

It was the type of course that enables you to look at what you don't like in your life and would like to change, and I am quite open to that. You learn about yourself and how you operate, on the basis that you can only work effectively with others when you know yourself.

Going to college made me see myself as an equal, a person in my own right with a voice that deserved to be heard as much as anybody else's. It made me realise that I wasn't stupid and didn't need special treatment.

Because I had all these new ideas about wanting to be my own person, I was keen to try them out, and it was a period in my life when my father didn't like me much. I became quite rebellious, especially in terms of seeing myself as *me* and not 'my father's daughter'. I think he found that rather hard, because he'd always pushed me to do certain things and here I was now almost saying: 'I don't need you any more. I can cope.'

I didn't realise what I was doing, I was unaware of how others might respond. Looking back, I think I could have handled some of it a bit more sensitively, but you don't always take a detached view at the time: you just do what you believe is right.

Those two years put an additional strain on our relationship and were very painful for both of us, because we love each other and are so alike in many ways. We are both quite pigheaded and strongwilled, and neither of us is 'big' enough to apologise to the other. After an argument I'd just storm off to the flat and say: 'That's it. I'm never going to talk to you again.' I can see now that it was very childish behaviour in some respects, and it went on till I was married. Usually it was Mum who would resolve the situation, phoning up afterwards to make sure I was OK.

I think I got too radical for Mum, too, although she understood better what I was going through because, like me, she is in the 'people' business. Dad thinks that most social work is bullshit: he doesn't believe in it. Being a practical person, he isn't used to the jargon people use, and the course made him feel a bit out of his depth.

When it came to our engagement, I didn't want Mark to ask my father for my 'hand' in marriage. I wanted both Mark and myself to tell my parents together that we planned to get married. After we had broken the news to them, all four of us went off for lunch at the Two Bridges, our local pub at Croxley Green. Mum and I wandered up to the bar to collect our lunch, leaving Dad and Mark to talk together before going to get *theirs*.

My father, apparently, told Mark: 'Alison is *your* responsibility now. Mind you look after her.' I'm glad I wasn't there to hear that! And when Dad mentioned later about 'giving me away' to Mark, I said to him: 'I'm not *yours* to give away.' We left those words out of the wedding service.

I think Dad was filled with two conflicting emotions about my marriage. He was pleased and happy that I would be 'looked after' (as he saw it), but at the same time he felt a deep sensė of loss. Until that point, he had imagined that he would always provide for me and be there for me. When another man comes into your daughter's life it must be difficult for any father to let go, and my disability probably made the letting go that much more poignant.

During the first year I was at college, Andy stayed in my flat for six months. Unfortunately, he nearly drove me crackers and we clashed a great deal. I am quite houseproud — not over the top, just liking a certain degree of tidiness — but Andy is an untidy person and he wouldn't help with the shopping.

I'd come back to the flat at weekends to find piles of dirty washing, mouldy bread in the bread bin and that stale smell of humans lingering about the place.

All the same, it was nice having him around for a while and a situation that no one had ever anticipated. Before that he'd always reckoned that I'd been handed things on a plate and never had to work for them. When I bought my first car out of my mobility allowance, he was quite envious and pissed off that *I* could do that while *he* had to go out and work for his car. But instead of being open with me and saying: 'Bloody hell! It's not fair,' he would make pointed little remarks several months later.

It was the same when I got my flat. He felt that my disability had given me an unfair advantage.

During my summer vacation in 1986, Mark and I worked together on a playscheme in Watford, run by my friend Cynthia from youth and community. We spent four weeks there and it was hard going, to say the least. Not only were we working alongside one another but living together in the flat as well, so we were seeing each other almost twenty-four hours a day.

But it was good fun. We had about a hundred and fifty kids on our books, all between the ages of seven and eleven, and roughly seventy were turning up each day. We did painting, games, stories, dressing up, craft — making junk models out of toilet rolls. There were four of us working together: Cynthia, Mo, Mark and me.

We were based in a community centre — a big old house containing several rooms, with different activities and groups in each, including an old people's club. The kids made cakes and we used to invite the old people in to a tea party.

Some days we took the kids to the park . . . and we all went on an outing by train to London Zoo. Most of them were of Pakistani origin and the trip happened to coincide with the Prophet's birthday, their Christmas Day.

It was the summer when I finally, reluctantly, became confirmed. The choice was a clearcut one: unless I was confirmed, I could not marry Mark. Once confirmed, I would then be a 'good Christian', liked and accepted by all the family and free to go ahead and plan our wedding.

Nevertheless, I continued to question and probe during my confirmation classes. I was curious about the whole concept of miracles, especially the kind where Jesus helps crippled people to walk. And my teacher and I enjoyed some fascinating discussions about the ordination of women which she, like me, supported.

In June 1986 my parents and Mark's parents met for the first time at my confirmation at St Stephen's House. I was confirmed at a private service there by the Archbishop of Wales, and most of the college attended.

At the end of Year One, I felt that I was coping, was getting my work handed in on time and had done well. Each of us did a self-assessment: you write it up, give it to your personal tutor and she/he writes a summary.

My attendance at lectures and tutorials had been faultless, but in Year Two it went a little haywire, mainly due to all the travelling. I had left the YMCA hostel and was back living in my flat at Rickmansworth again (Andy was now back with Mum and Dad). Thanks to the newly completed M25, I was able to commute to college, but it took me an hour and a half each way (fifty minutes if the traffic was lighter).

At the beginning of my second year people were sent on placements, and after the summer vacation you went straight to your placement. In my case it was Winchester, where I spent three months. Other students were based in Scotland, Wales, the Midlands . . .

Winchester taught me a lot about myself. I knew nobody at all there, so it was up to me to find out about accommodation and locate the tutor who had been assigned to me — a woman called Hilary Robinson, who worked in the local YMCA.

I found digs in the YWCA, a very old, rambling house in a

small village with a church and a few shops, not far from the city centre. About twenty-five of us lived there, women and men. Duncan and Mark drove me down there in two cars full of my stuff: my music (tapes, cassette player), clothes, college files, typewriter, photos, and not forgetting Winnie, my pet mascot.

I arrived with Mark and Duncan in tow. We unloaded the cars and carried all my things into my new room, which had two single beds in it. I remember looking around and thinking: 'I've got to be here for *three months*!' — and I felt so lonely, and frightened. A great wave of panic at being left alone overwhelmed me. Whenever I start in a new area, I always experience a feeling of not being able to cope.

I can recall walking down to the car park with Mark and Duncan and not wanting Mark to go. I was in tears watching them drive off and I thought: 'For goodness' sake, Alison, pull yourself together.'

I went back upstairs to my room and decided to unpack and try to make it look like *my* room. I spent most of the evening up there getting it looking nice and lived-in. It was all self-catering, so after a while I went into the kitchen to cook myself a meal: baked beans on toast. I thought to myself: 'I can't live on beans on toast for the next three months!'

One night I met Tom, who was resident there. He was gay. He'd come down from Liverpool to find work and had a job in the local hospital. We hit it off straight away, and something told me that he might be gay. As soon as he could see that I had no hangups on that score, he was able to speak quite freely with me about it and we ended up close friends.

I fell in love with Winchester. It's a beautiful city and I loved the shopping area — spent a lot of time shopping . . . I'm the type of person who, if I'm feeling down, goes and buys herself a goody.

*

My project entailed testing out what I had learned during the previous year at college, and I was set four tasks: 1) community studies; 2) management and administration; 3) working with individuals; 4) group work. These are the four basic areas that every youth worker should know about.

1. Community studies: this was very much a study of the whole community, which was the village where I lived. Where people went to work, how many owned their own homes, how many lived in council houses, what facilities were available for youngsters (were there any mother and toddler clubs?). Was it an affluent area? Was there much vandalism? (etc).

2. Management and administration: this involved finding out how the YMCA's financial system worked; how to manage staff, committees, membership; how to run a building on a day-to-day basis. This was useful and helps me in my present job as a youth worker.

3. Working with individuals: I had to pick an individual young person and assess the kinds of areas where I felt I could help them develop. (I chose a young girl.)

4. Group work: the part I liked best. I was working with a group of about eight sixteen-year-old youths, and I can remember one incident where they were giving me some hassle. They were upstairs in the YMCA coffee bar, looking down at me as I was walking outside. I could see them all sitting in a circle staring out the window and making fun. As I entered the building I heard one of them say: 'Here comes the spastic.' I told myself to ignore it, but when I went up to the coffee bar I decided to confront them. The other part-time workers obviously felt uncomfortable at what was taking place and unsure of what to do.

'Here we go,' I thought, and taking a deep breath I said: 'If you want to take the piss do it in front of me and not behind my back . . . OK?' There was a dead silence. All of them remained very much on the defensive.

'Look, I have a disability,' I said. 'I've got CP. I can sit here and talk about it if you want.' Pause. 'Well, what's CP then?' someone asked. I went on to explain. I avoid the term 'brain damage' because kids tend to pick up on it and say: 'Does that mean your brain doesn't work?'

Afterwards, the other workers came up to me and said: 'Well done. That must have taken some real "bottle".' And it does — because I don't *enjoy* hostility or ill feeling. With me, head-on confrontation is what works best. It's just one of the ways I cope in that kind of situation. I say: 'If you want to know what is wrong with me, *ask*,' — and nine times out of ten they will ask, and that is when I am able to get a discussion going. I teach them what CP is about, and that knocks down barriers and helps build up relationships.

Once they know what is the matter, kids can become quite protective of you. It is interesting that long after I left Winchester and lost contact with this particular group, they were still asking people how I was and what I was doing.

Winchester is not all that far from Oxford, and every third weekend I drove there to see Mark. My two years at the YMCA college were a good test of our relationship. We were both away all week in separate institutions, studying hard, short of money, going through personal change, and coming together with new ideas to discuss. I don't know, looking back, how we made it through that time, but we did — and the bond between us grew stronger as a result.

I also had to prepare my dissertation. For my theme I chose 'Sex and the Disabled', as I had become increasingly aware of the widespread lack of knowledge and information on the subject. I went into schools and colleges and interviewed head teachers, care staff, pupils, parents.

Many people were reluctant to speak openly to me, which made it a very tricky assignment for me. Disabled people themselves confirmed my worst fears: that in special schools and institutions there is no privacy, no provision for sex education at all, no 'space' given to learn or practise sexual behaviour, and no counselling facilities to help them cope with their emotions.

The care staff in colleges for the disabled are not trained to deal with sexual or emotional needs. They feel embarrassed about putting disabled people into bed with each other, but they could be trained to deal with this. What right have they to deny anybody a sexual experience in this way? To say: 'No, I will not lift you out of your chair and into X's bed,' is wrong. It is penalising that person because of their disability.

What I did find is that this denial tends to be linked with an able-bodied person's view of their own sexuality: unless they are in tune with their sexuality, they feel uncomfortable about coping with other people's.

From my researches I concluded that although I felt the situation was beginning to improve, 'it is only part of a wider acceptance in Society which must occur before disabled people are seen as sexual beings'.

I'm not an expert, but I feel that more needs to be done to counsel carers, parents and teachers on this subject as they are the ones who are doing the denying.

Sex and the disabled is still a taboo area. I suppose it goes back to Mark, who had to get over his fear of touching *me* as a sexual being. It's like when he first kissed me on the forehead. He probably wondered: 'Can she kiss properly? Will she respond?'

I've made myself unpopular with certain parties, such as some people who worked for the Spastics Society, who say that I shouldn't be going around encouraging disabled people to have sex before marriage. They thought that I overstepped the mark in one talk I gave to a group of social workers some time ago. You hear things through the grapevine. People ring you and say: 'I liked the talk/film, but that was a bit *strong*, wasn't it?' But *somebody* needs to be outspoken, because most people haven't a clue what goes on in institutions.

My father has always said: 'Say what you believe.' *He* does, and I think I get it from him.

I do get myself into a lot of trouble, and this is one of my problems: when I feel passionately about something, I can't let it go. It can be both a strength and a weakness. If you don't know when to stop, others may get fed up with you and won't listen. On the other hand, if you don't challenge things you believe to be wrong, you feel bad inside.

Mark and I had to go and see the Bishop of Swansea and Brecon about getting married. Having given his formal consent, he then asked me about my work and I told him about the course I was doing at the YMCA college, mentioning that I would have to work abroad for a month as a condition of the course. Swansea and Brecon are twinned with the diocese of Wyoming in the USA and the Bishop suggested some names of contacts out there, mainly children's homes. I wrote to several of these and around Easter 1987 ended up working in a cathedral home in Laramie for children who had been sexually and mentally abused.

It was a kind of halfway house where they could stay for a maximum of twelve months, and it involved a re-training programme, mainly one to one but also group sessions run by a wonderful woman called Robin, from whom I learned a lot.

They were hard, streetwise kids aged from twelve to seventeen. Each one had their own programme, aims and goals to meet. Eventually, some were reunited with their families; others were fostered or adopted.

I found it quite a traumatic, highly charged experience, and I was struck by how difficult it was to build relationships with these young people, because they seemed to show so little *trust*.

Mark came with me and we stayed with the Dean of Wyoming, his wife Shirley and daughter Mollie in their large four-bedroomed house in Laramie in the State of Wyoming.

One day we went flying with the Bishop of Wyoming in his own four-seater aeroplane. The Bishop asked Mark if he would like to take over the controls. I was sitting in the back, thinking: 'Please — no!' We were wobbling a bit and at about five thousand feet the Bishop suggested that Mark might like to 'straighten her out'. Suddenly, the tail of the plane shot up and I felt so ill. They heard me groaning in the back: 'I think perhaps I'd better take over again, Mark,' the Bishop said.

We were up there for about half an hour. Unlike Mark, I did *not* enjoy this experience.

Both of us put on loads of weight from all the gargantuan pancake breakfasts and brunches, and we met some lovely people, who really made us welcome. Mollie, the Dean's daughter, introduced us to several of her friends and we explored some of the neighbourhood bars together. My disability was not a problem in Wyoming. People there seemed much more accepting of disability. As in Canada, their access to buildings was wonderful and a great improvement on ours in Britain. There were 'Ask for Help' signs and most public buildings, such as banks and libraries, had ramps.

Wyoming was like a period of suspended animation, a block of concentrated time together, and that was very important to us then. It was only about ten weeks until our wedding, and as soon as we got home the mad rush began. I was finding all the commuting in and out of London a great strain, and I felt too tired to socialise.

There were weeks when we didn't talk much, and the closer it came to Mark's exams the more edgy he became. He churns himself up inside with worry and I had to be careful what I said.

I remember one massive row we had. Duncan (our best man) was there at the time, and Mark said something to me like: 'When we're married you'll be mine.' I was so angry I flung my engagement ring on to the floor, stormed into my room and slammed the door.

I'd had to alter my anti-marriage views in the light of my relationship with a future priest. I knew there was no way I could have lived with Mark, as a priest, without being married. Neither the Church nor the people in the parish would have accepted the situation.

We knew we wanted to be together, but I felt insecure about moving to Wales, which was such a long way from home. In Watford I'd been used to a congenial, convenient set-up: friends, my parents — and guaranteed job security. SW Herts had promised to re-employ me as a part-time worker after my college course was finished. To forgo all those advantages, those certainties, and to move to Wales where I knew nobody, was not an easy decision for me to make.

Deep down, though, I never doubted my love for Mark. It just didn't occur to me that our relationship could fail. We knew we were right for each other. 'Made in heaven,' as Mark says! I don't know if I agree with that, but it keeps him happy!

10

I Get Mentioned — and Married — by the Bishop

Mark and I were keen to marry as soon as possible after we'd finished college so that we could both start life in the Treboeth parish in Swansea together as a team. As we neared the end of our final terms, all the wedding preparations were getting under way. Tensions were building up and people's nerves becoming over-stretched. I was still living in my flat, commuting to college, trying to finish my dissertation *and* join in all the goodbye parties. Mark was still in Oxford and slowly getting used to the fact that after seven years of studying and dossing around he would actually have to start working for a living.

Mum and I were busy sorting out arrangements for the bridesmaids (Laura and Louise Davies, daughters of my friend Cynthia, whom I'd met on the same training weekend as Mark. Laura is our god-daughter), flowers, cake, my hair, my shoes, and The Dress. We looked at hundreds of dresses, some with ridiculously inflated prices, and the endless trying-on made me feel dizzy.

Mum and I were in hysterics trying to choose the right shoes. It took us ages. We couldn't find any that were remotely suitable, and we had visions of me walking up the aisle in wellington boots! There was a basic choice between high heels or sling backs, neither of which I could keep on my feet. About two weeks before the wedding we found a pair that fitted and then they weren't brilliant.

If I'd had my way about the dress I wouldn't have worn a veil, and instead of a long white dress I'd have chosen a red one. But I thought: 'No, you can't do that to Mum.' Plus the fact that if you marry a priest you have to be a bit circumspect.

So we came to certain compromises, but I did have my own way, in — for instance — deciding on the kind of reception, and in not having Dad 'give me away'. The word 'obey' went, too (I promised to love and honour, but obey was deleted).

In the middle of all the pre-wedding panic, a removal firm arrived at the flat to pick up all my stuff. Before that, we'd had to bring all Mark's belongings down from Oxford to my flat, and now the removal men came and emptied the place completely, transporting the contents to our new home in Swansea.

For about a month before our wedding I was living back with my parents. I was still at college when Mark went on retreat for a week, as part of his preparation for ordination. I was rather peeved that he should have gone and left me in the midst of all this hassle and thought he could have timed things a bit better!

Before Mark's ordination, my best mate Cynthia and her two little girls came down to the house in Swansea with me. Then my parents arrived. Things were pretty chaotic, as it's only a small house. My parents slept upstairs in our bedroom. Cynthia, Laura and myself slept on the couch downstairs, with Louise curled up in an armchair.

On the Sunday we all travelled up in my car to Brecon for Mark's ordination at the cathedral. Mark was ordained by Bishop Benjamin, the Bishop of Swansea and Brecon, who also married us three weeks later. It was a two-hour ceremony, and I wore a trendy black and white striped, tracksuit-style outfit with matching socks, shoes and triangular earrings. I stood out among the hats and floral dresses. It must be the childish part of me that feels compelled to shock people all the time. Hopefully, they are so preoccupied with what I am wearing that they forget about my disability.

The Bishop mentioned me in his sermon. I was sitting in the front pew and he waved to me and I waved back. Everyone took the piss out of me about it afterwards. 'Oh, mentioned by the *Bishop*, were you, Alison?' I'm very fond of Bishop Benjamin — or Binnie, as he is known to his friends.

After his ordination Mark returned to Swansea to work in the parish for a couple of weeks before we were married.

My father tunes the piano belonging to Jean Groome who writes for the *Watford Observer*, and she was very interested to hear about my forthcoming wedding and asked if she could write an article on us. We agreed to this. Then she phoned up Ann Paul (producer of *Forty Minutes*) and told her that I was getting married. Ann then rang *me*. I realised that once Ann knew about my wedding there would be a good chance of another film being made.

About two days before the wedding a full film crew arrived. Ann Paul sat on the sofa in the living room with Mark and myself doing a full interview with us both. Afterwards we discussed arrangements for filming the wedding itself. It was all rather tightly packed together as time was getting short.

Mark then went off to Duncan's (our best man) where he was staying the night before the wedding. I remained at home with my parents. I remember phoning Mark on our wedding morning just to see how he felt and he said: 'Well, *I*'m all right, but Duncan is a bag of nerves.' So I said: 'For goodness' sake calm him down.' Mark and I had built the whole thing up beforehand, making out that he, Duncan, was going to be the star. We'd pretended that they were going to record his entire speech and he was worried about all the TV cameras being there.

We were married at All Saints Church, Croxley Green, on July 11, 1987, at 2.0 p.m. Duncan, Mark and some of the concelebrating priests had arrived at the church quite early. Meanwhile, the two bridesmaids and myself had been at the hairdressers at 10.0 a.m. Sue, my regular stylist from Total Look, did my hair. Some of the other clients gave me wedding cards and the whole mood there was just lovely.

Two o'clock got closer. Christopher, the page boy (Mark's second cousin) arrived, the bridesmaids got dressed, *I* got dressed . . . Then it was just me and Dad left in the house and I was saying: 'Dad, do I look all right?' . . . 'Are you *sure*?'

When I opened the front door and walked out on to the pavement Ann Paul was standing there. That made me smile, because Ann seems to be at every big event in my life. Wherever the action is, Ann is bound to be around.

She followed me and Dad to the church. When we arrived I had to stand to one side to make way for the Bishop and the concelebrating priests, one of whom was Mark's college friend. Binnie stopped to give me a kiss before he went into the church, followed by all the priests.

Then I heard the opening notes of our first hymn, 'Our God Reigns', and my tummy did a leap. I stood in front of the big wooden door feeling as if I was about to faint. Every single emotion went through my body, and I remember following this long procession of priests in their robes to the altar, and thinking: 'He'd better be there waiting. If he's not, I'll kill him.' But he *was* there, and as soon as he turned round and I saw his great beaming face, I knew everything was going to be all right.

The service was in the form of a nuptial mass with incense, communion, the whole ritual. Wonderful! I'd left the choice of most hymns to Mark and he set out the wedding service in a small booklet.

Everybody sang so well, the bridesmaids were brilliant, it was great. About three hundred people were present, including seven priests, the Bishop, a deacon and a full television crew. BBC TV's *Forty Minutes* team were there and they included extracts from the service in their most recent film about me, which went out in March 1988. To be honest, I hardly noticed the lights or the cameras. I was much too wrapped up in the magical excitement of the occasion, floating away in my own private world. Certain parts of the mass I just don't remember at all. I was seeing them through a kind of haze.

Ann Paul and I had worked it all out in advance so that the cameras would be as unobtrusive as possible. She and her team knew how important it was for them to co-operate with Mark and myself over this. After all, I was only planning to get married once, with no re-takes!

Afterwards, when I was walking back down the aisle with Mark, people were looking so happy and it was nice to see their smiling faces. We went into the garden and had loads of pictures taken, which seemed to take ages.

Then Mark and I were driven to the reception at Watersmeet, a leisure centre in Rickmansworth with various function rooms and a bar. We had invited eighty guests, and we both stood at the top end of the room shaking everyone's hand as they came in and introducing them to our families. We mingled for a while before sitting down to a three-course dinner, a lovely meal consisting of a starter of soup or fruit juice, followed by the main dish of roast chicken, roast potatoes and vegetables, and a sweet of black forest gateau or fruit salad. With champagne, of course.

Then we moved on to the speeches. Duncan did his bit, and I watched the cameras zooming in on him. 'Poor bloke,' I thought. He was so nervous, but he did very, very well.

Mark said a few words, followed by Dad, and then me. I just thanked the bridesmaids; Cynthia, their mum (for helping to see me through it all); Mark's mum (for making the cake); and John, a friend, who organised the evening disco (his wedding present to us).

The cameras were around all the time, but the crew were very considerate and kept in the background.

We had a short honeymoon: two nights in expensive hotels. Duncan and Simon Fricker had booked us into the Windsor Castle Hotel — it was *their* treat. Mark drove us there in my old Datsun, which they had ruined with tin cans, bog paper, red balloons, and shaving cream on the windscreen announcing 'Rev and Wife', which ate into the paintwork.

We were shown to our room, and there facing us was a beautiful, enormous four-poster bed, together with a bottle of champagne and a box of chocolates. We got undressed and into bed, looking forward to our champagne. Mark undid the foil, the cork went up, the bottle went down . . . and all we had left was about a glass of the stuff between us. We just couldn't stop laughing.

In the morning we had a lovely traditional English cooked breakfast, brought to us in bed on a silver tray.

Later that day we drove on to Marlborough and visited the village of Avebury, where we saw the famous Neolithic stones of Avebury Circle. We spent our second night in the Ivy House Hotel, Marlborough. The weather was perfect and the following morning we sat outside our hotel room and ate breakfast on the verandah.

They were the two best nights of my life. We couldn't stay away any longer as we had to return to the new house in

Swansea. There were still masses of boxes and cases to unpack, not to mention all the wedding presents.

I wouldn't mind repeating the actual wedding day, but not the preparations, which were a nightmare. I knew, though, that once we were married there would be no more weeks apart, no more long separations. We would always be together.

After our wedding we settled into the parsonage, our new house in Swansea. Ann Paul phoned me soon after we arrived and said she needed to do some more filming in order to make a *Forty Minutes* documentary. So she came down with the film crew and over a period of about six months Mark and I just lived our lives with the crew. The idea was that if I knew that anything exciting was about to happen in my life I would ring Ann and she would turn up to film it.

When I applied for a job at Neath YMCA, I duly phoned Ann and told her when I had an interview lined up. At first I wasn't sure whether or not I wanted her to be there as I didn't want the presence of the cameras to influence the outcome, but after talking it over with her on the phone, we agreed that if they just filmed me going in and coming out afterwards, and not the actual interview, that would work OK. So Ann phoned the YMCA and cleared it all with them.

The appointment in question was that of General Secretary. It was a post which was a little above my head, but I was keen to go for it even so. I was shortlisted out of quite a number of applicants, and I was pleased about that.

The interview lasted about an hour, and I don't think I've ever worked so hard in my life. I felt completely wrung out afterwards, though I also felt that I'd acquitted myself well.

Unfortunately, I failed to get the job, and that upset me at first, but I soon bounced back. I simply hadn't had the kind of experience they needed.

Ann also showed me giving talks to the local junior school, which I've been doing on and off for a while now.

I was also filmed shopping with Mark, and in other situations, all aimed at portraying my new life in Swansea, which was totally different from the life I'd known in Watford.

After it was over and the film had been edited, Mark and I went up to London to see the preview. We travelled up to Kensington House (a BBC TV building) near Shepherd's Bush, where we met Ann again and watched the film. Mark was nearly in tears and I felt quite emotional.

To coincide with *I, Alison* (in the *Forty Minutes* series), which was due to be shown on March 9, 1988, I was talked into doing *Wogan*. I felt apprehensive about appearing on a live, prime time programme, but one of the researchers came to Swansea and we discussed the whole thing — how I would cope generally, and what sort of questions would be asked.

We caught the train to London, all expenses paid, and stayed in the Kensington Hilton Hotel (near Shepherd's Bush). Mark fell in love with this hotel because in our bedroom we had one of those automatic gin and tonic machines which works at the push of a button.

When we arrived at the BBC TV Theatre on Shepherd's Bush Green, I was literally trembling at the knees, thinking: 'Bloody hell, Alison, what are you doing here?' We were ushered around like VIPs. First, we were shown into the Hospitality room, where we met actor Robert Hardy. We chatted to him for a while, then I had to go into Makeup for about half an hour.

I met the other guests: Matthew Taylor, the youngest (Liberal) MP in the House of Commons; and the pop group, Aha, who were too preoccupied with their fans to notice us.

The worst part for me was sitting in Hospitality, watching the monitor screens, hearing the music (from Aha) and knowing that I was due on next. I must have gone to the toilet about ten times.

Then it came to my turn. The floor manager came to meet Mark and myself and escorted us down to the wings. I stood there with him while the group was singing, and I felt this sheer panic attack coming on. It was too late for another trip to the loo, and before I knew it we were on air.

I'd never done a live broadcast before and I knew that *Wogan* was high in the ratings. Sue Lawley was standing in for Terry Wogan, who was on leave, and she succeeded in putting me at my ease.

Later, back in Hospitality, I enjoyed myself talking to people and having drinks, but before — and during — I was terrified.

We got back to our hotel at about nine o'clock and went straight into the restaurant for dinner. People kept looking at us and saying: 'She was on *Wogan*,' 'We saw you on *Wogan*.' It was amazing the number of people who recognised us.

After we had eaten we felt shattered and went to bed. We spent the next day exploring London and we popped over to see my parents in Watford as well. Then all of us, including Mum and Dad, drove to Ann Paul's house, where we had a party to celebrate *I, Alison* which was being shown that night. Loads of people were at the party: Eddie Mirzoeff (ex-Editor of *Forty Minutes*) camera crew, sound people, researchers, Ann's family, my parents . . .

When it was time for the film to begin, we all went downstairs and crammed into a little television room in the basement and watched in absolute silence. As soon as it had finished everyone clapped like crazy. Ann's telephone started to ring, with friends and colleagues congratulating her on the film.

The following day I was booked to do *Open Air* in Manchester. Mark, Ann and I had to be on the road by 7.0 a.m. to get to Gatwick Airport to fly there in time for the programme at 11.0 a.m. We arrived at the airport about 7.30 a.m. All three of us were walking towards the departure gate minding our own business, but people were stopping us to say: 'We saw you on telly. Well done!' We were staggered at the numbers who waylaid us: it felt as if every other person we passed had seen me on *Wogan* — or had seen the film.

We had breakfast on the plane. We'd bought all the newspapers to read the reviews, and all of them were good except for the one from *The Times* (I think *he* may have had a problem about disability himself). It was strange to watch yourself on TV one night and the next day to realise that half of England had seen you too! I began to feel like a real celebrity. I said to Ann: 'It's all your fault, you know!' and she just laughed.

Ann was going to appear on the programme with me. Now, Ann is fine behind the camera, but when she gets in front she doesn't feel comfortable. She has the same sort of reaction to nerves as I have and so, as we got nearer the studio, we both started dashing towards the loo.

Open Air is a programme where viewers ring in live and ask questions. Again, I had never done anything like this before and I was quite worried about the kinds of questions people might ask. No one briefed me beforehand. Apparently, the lines had been jammed with calls since the previous night: the biggest response they'd ever had to any programme. I was delighted.

Most of the questions centred on ways in which I coped with my disability, but one or two were more unusual. One woman phoned and said: 'If you ever divorce Mark, can I have him?' I was so taken aback by this that I said: 'Yes, I'll send him to you.' Then she said: 'Well, can you do it first class because I don't want him fractured!' I could hear Mark cracking up laughing behind the scenes.

The question which stands out most in my mind was: how did I feel about not getting the job at Neath YMCA? I replied: 'I wasn't good enough.' This guy had got so *involved* with the events in the *Forty Minutes* programme and he really wanted me to get that job.

Afterwards, we went to Hospitality, where we met the producer, who was very pleased at how well the programme had gone. Then Mark and I were driven all the way back to Swansea, but I don't remember much about it. We'd both used up so much emotional energy that we slept throughout the entire journey.

Next, I was asked to do *Going Live*, a three-hour children's programme which goes out on BBC TV on Saturday mornings, with Sarah Greene and Philip Schofield. Once again, Mark and I stayed at the Kensington Hilton Hotel. When we went down for our meal the night before the show, the restaurant manager — who knew us by name from last time — came over to welcome us. 'Alison, come and sit over here,' he said.

Mark's brother, Paul, and his girlfriend, Claudia, were with us and were well impressed by all the attention we were getting. We all sat and enjoyed a marvellous meal, waiters everywhere, waiting on us hand and foot. It was quite funny.

On the Saturday morning we did *Going Live*, and I had a great time, though my nerves hadn't improved. I'm just as tense and worried each time I appear on TV.

I was in the Hot Seat and had to answer questions about disability from kids in the studio audience. Mark was watching from behind the scenes. I was on between the pop videos, cartoons and various guests, who included Jason Donovan, alias Scott in *Neighbours*.

I was getting so much feedback from all the programmes,

so many positive spin-offs. After the first showing of *I, Alison* (it was repeated within a month due to popular demand), our neighbourhood seemed to be buzzing with people who knew us or wanted to know us. We had more than three hundred letters from viewers, the phone was always ringing, and shopping was impossible as we kept being stopped in Sainsbury's.

Unfortunately, not everyone we came across showed an enlightened response. Judging by their behaviour towards me, some people seem to have missed the whole point of the programme. When Mark and I went to the Royal Welsh (agricultural) Show at Builth Wells in June 1988, about ninety per cent of people addressed their remarks to him, not to me, congratulating Mark on the 'wonderful' film and my 'terrific' sense of humour . . . and I was standing right next to him!

Mark gets bloody angry as well, though he doesn't show it. He is able to channel his feelings, to conceal them under a veneer of politeness. He will say: 'This is Alison, my wife,' 'she's *here*, you know', pointedly bringing me into the conversation.

It is OK for a while and I can handle it. If I were to suddenly start shouting and screaming it would achieve nothing and might even turn them against disabled people completely. But I find their attitude depressing, because I believe my role is to educate people about disability, and when that kind of situation occurs I think: 'Why do I do it? Why put myself through so much pain?'

When I start a new job, for the first month or so I know the kids will take the piss out of me because I am different. Although it hurts and upsets me, I believe that if I can work through this with them and they are able to learn from me, it might make it easier for other disabled people to be accepted in society.

11

Managing in Swansea

I felt quite anxious about moving to Wales because, to me, it was a completely new country and, although I'd been there on holiday, I'd never stayed there for longer than two weeks. I was worried, too, as I knew that some Welsh people didn't like the English and wasn't sure if that applied to the Swansea area . . . but I loved Mark and Mark happened to be Welsh, so it was a case of: 'Look out, Wales, here we come!'

We live in a two-up-two-down semi, with a small garden, on a new estate about three miles outside Swansea. The parish is called Treboeth, and it is situated on a hill, so getting around can be quite difficult for me at times. Behind our house are some large open fields, where I am able to take our two dogs (Megan and Dottie) for walks. Dottie was a wedding present and I bought Megan from the Swansea Dogs' home.

There are two churches in our parish: the main one, which is St Albans, and the daughter church (Penlan), so Mark is kept very busy. Father Douglas Davies is our vicar.

I felt lonely at first but found the people in the congregation very welcoming and friendly towards me. They went out of their way to make me feel comfortable. On Sunday evenings Mark and I run a youth club in the church hall where we all play table tennis, or just chat and enjoy a good laugh together. It's nice to see so many young people with a strong religious belief.

When we first came to Swansea, I didn't have a job, and so I took quite an active part in parish life: going to coffee mornings, giving lifts to old people, visiting them in their homes . . . It was a way of enabling me to get to know local parishioners.

But we made it perfectly clear that I'm not the flower-arranging, church-cleaning type. I'm not there for that. I'm there as Mark's partner. I will go to functions with him, I have helped with the occasional church jumble sale and I don't mind taking the old folk to hospital or church, because I can do that sort of thing on my own without getting too involved. But I refuse to be manipulated into doing what other people *think* I should do.

In November 1987 I attended my graduation ceremony at the YMCA headquarters in London. I was over the moon. I wanted to cry and laugh all at once because, although I knew I'd passed, I still wanted to feel that precious piece of paper in my grubby little hands!

This might sound bigheaded — but I'm the only one in my family with a professional qualification, and to have achieved that and to know that I did it on my own, means so much to me.

My relationship with my brother Andy changed after I got married. He suddenly realised: 'She is independent now. She doesn't need me any longer.' He would no longer have to think about 'looking after me' in the future: that pressure was removed from him.

Shortly after the *Forty Minutes* film had been transmitted, I went on a course called the All Wales Strategy Course, geared to carers and teachers who worked with mentally handicapped people. I was asked along to see if I would be interested in becoming a tutor.

Around that time a social worker who had seen the programme telephoned me and asked if I would like to help run a mentally handicapped group on Monday and Tuesday evenings. I wasn't keen, but I knew it would be good experience for my future employment, as it would show that I was actively trying to find work. So I did it for about six months but was rather put off by the fact that the parents treated *me* as a mentally handicapped person, too.

Then, I had to have my appendix out, which knocked me back for a while. I went back to help once or twice after I was better, but soon stopped altogether.

I also met a woman called Katreen Donaldson, who used to work with the Family Planning Association in Swansea and was now a freelance tutor, working in conjunction with the government's Employment Training (ET) scheme. Katreen is in her early forties, a wonderful and very 'together' person. She asked me if I'd also like to be involved, and I said: 'Yes.'

In June 1988, twelve months after his ordination as deacon, Mark attended his ordination as priest, again at Brecon Cathedral. This ordination is similar except that, as well as the Bishop, priests from the diocese also lay hands on you, so that you are all sharing in a kind of common ministry. My parents came down for the occasion. Mark came forward in his cassock and alb and knelt in front of the Bishop. His father then came forward and they both laid hands on Mark's head. His mum was very moved, and I had to hold back the tears as I knew how much all this meant to Mark.

A few days after Mark's 'priesting' (ordination) he took his first mass, a communion service in the form of a modern folk mass, presided over by Mark, together with concelebrating priests, including his father, who also preached, and several priests from St Stephen's House including the Principal and the parish priest.

I sat at the front with all Mark's family. I felt extremely nervous, knowing that it was the first time Mark had ever said mass, but he did very well.

Having been turned down for the job at Neath YMCA, I then heard about another vacancy — for a job based at the local girls' comprehensive school: leader of a youth wing attached to Mynyddbach County Girls' School. As soon as I knew it was up for grabs I went to visit and I could see so much potential there. I can remember coming home and thinking: 'It's wonderful. I want it!'

So I filled in the form and sent it off. It took me a long time for my application to be processed. What they didn't tell me at this stage was that there were not enough applicants to select somebody for the job. I kept on phoning up to try and find out what was happening but no one was telling me.

Several weeks later I received a letter saying that my application was being re-submitted. The job had been readvertised and I ended up on a shortlist of six.

The interview was an all-day affair in front of an all-male panel. They wrote down their questions so that these would be the same for everybody. I knew my subject and felt pretty confident that I was in with a good chance.

In the afternoon I was told that the job was mine. It was exhilarating to think that I had gone to college, got qualified and landed myself a full-time job — and in a strange new place, where I wasn't known.

When I drove home Mark was looking out of the window for me. As soon as I saw him I gave him the thumbs-up and we both stood in the front garden bawling our eyes out.

I started work at Mynyddbach in August 1988. On my first

morning my boss, Andy Pudduck, with some of the blokes at the youth wing, showed me round and gave me the keys, and we went out to lunch together.

A week or so later school started back, and I met all the kids. Then I was introduced to my fourteen part-time workers, who are wonderful. I couldn't run the club without them, and they have been very supportive towards me as their new leader. Now and again they have 'digs' about my being English, but there's been no real problem.

My boss, Andy, has also been extremely supportive, and I have supervision with him once a week.

I'm in charge of maintaining and managing the building. I also have to pay and supervise my part-time staff. It is very much a manager's role with youth work attached. The managing bit I do because I have to — I get paid for it — but I regard myself basically as a youth worker, not a desk worker. I get so much from face-to-face contact with youngsters. About a hundred and twenty kids come through my doors each day and I have to try and make time for every one of them.

People say to me: 'Do you *work*?'

'Yes,' I say.

'Got a part-time job, have you?'

'No,' I tell them. 'It's full-time, with a helluva lot of responsibility.'

I can see myself staying put either until I grow out of the job, or until Mark has to move to his next curacy. That prospect does worry me, because it took me twelve months to find this job and I don't know if I could wait that long again.

I really enjoy my work. It adds something to my life and makes me more independent.

Teenagers are very impressionable, which is why youth work suits me so well. They can see that although I have problems I am still able to get on with my life and help them.

Parents can make a real mess of your life: I feel that very strongly. When I'm out shopping I notice kids looking at me and I can hear their parents say: 'Don't stare. It's rude.' Or: 'She's not very well.' I think to myself: 'For goodness' sake, just *tell* them!'

Parents' prejudices rub off on to their children. You then get a vicious circle which I like to believe I am here to break. I think the more people I can touch through education, the better.

I don't work well with disabled people. Maybe I'm being selfish but I get frustrated and impatient and want them to help themselves more. I feel that they cop out and say to themselves: 'Society expects me to be useless, so that's what I'll be.' This attitude is evident even in the childish way in which some of them dress: twenty-year-old women with bunches in their hair and wearing frilly frocks.

I'm aware that not everybody has my determination or motivation, but individually and given enough support, I believe they could do more for themselves.

I don't believe in positive discrimination. To say that because a person is disabled they should have special treatment, is wrong. I just think that everybody should be given the same opportunities and judged on their own merits. My tutor from the YMCA National College, Peter Harding, wrote this in a testimonial about me: 'Alison has won her independence and self respect without special treatment and on her own efforts.'

Basically, I don't like to conform, and that's another reason why I enjoy youth work so much: young kids dislike conforming and I can identify with them in that. If somebody wants to go around with pink hair and bright green trousers, why can't they?

If I think that I might shock somebody, then I will go all out to do it — like at Mark's ordination as deacon, when I turned up in my black and white jogging suit. Everyone was oohing and aahing, because it was just not *done* . . . but I did it!

Mark has always been noisy, outgoing, very Welsh. He didn't change when he met me. He still smokes but rarely in the house—he usually enjoys a cigar or pipe in his little shed in the back garden, where I'm not allowed. Neither of us will change, whether we are meeting people in the parish or the Queen Mother. We muck around in public and slag each other off. We are both quite tactile people and some of the older ones find this hard to accept. They feel uncomfortable, with us being so open, honest and loving with one another.

When we go to church on Sundays we walk in together, Mark in his cassock and me in my multi-coloured patchwork jeans. Then we make our way up the aisle together, he kisses me goodbye and they all *look* . . . I stay in my pew at the front, while Mark goes up to the altar to do his bit.

I go to mass every Sunday morning. The main reason I go is to support Mark. Sometimes I feel hypocritical about sitting there in church and about taking communion. I don't seem to get this 'inner peace' feeling that other people speak about. Someone once asked me how I was feeling *spiritually*, and I didn't know what they meant. I guess I'm just too logical.

As to the actual role of 'curate's wife' (I hate that term: it's never 'the social worker's husband'!), I enjoy it because I like mixing with people and helping them out. I try to combine the two sides of my life as I think it's important that people know that I have a job and can only give a certain amount of my time to parish work. But I will always support Mark. If ever he needs me I'll be there—and I know he feels the same about me.

Ours is not a stereotyped marriage. Mark does his fair share in the home, and I do mine. We both have full-time jobs, so why should one person take on all the responsibility for the domestic chores?

I'd like two or three kids, but I certainly don't intend giving up work. Mark knows that and he wouldn't want me to. He knows how much my job means to me. In any case, we can't afford it (Mark gets £6,500 a year as a curate; I earn around £9,000 as a youth leader).

Having children is something we've talked long and hard about. Mark is very capable and willing to do everything apart from breast feeding! If I had a baby it would probably be by Caesarian, as I may not have enough physical strength to push.

The chances of my having a disabled child are minimal. CP isn't catching! But I'm not sure how I would cope with a disabled child — knowing exactly what they were going through, realising what other people were thinking. My expectations of the child would be very high: it would be 'normal' schools, 'normal' everything, and I don't know whether that's fair on the child.

I've always been a fighter, battling against the odds, breaking out of my stereotype, and yet plenty of people still put me down and I find that very soul-destroying.

I've changed in the way that I look at my disability. Although I still don't accept it I can see positive ways in which I can use it to my advantage — to educate and make contact with young people in a club situation. If I can't perform a particular task I will ask someone to help out. Nine times out of ten they will agree to do it, and that creates communication between us.

I feel I have got better since I married — much stronger than before, because I am doing so many different things. I am holding down a full-time job which I used to think I would never have the energy to do. I am always up and out on Sunday mornings, whereas I used to stay in bed. My disability doesn't seem to hold me back any more. It could be an attitude of my mind that makes me feel like this. Part of the secret is in planning your day sensibly and not cramming too much into it. At work I delegate a lot . . . and when I come home at lunchtime after a morning's work (I work in the evenings from 6.30 until 9.0 p.m. too), I have a cup of tea, turn on the telly and go to sleep.

The point behind this book is not: 'Look how well I've done. Aren't I clever?' My main aim is to try to dispel the image of disabled people as helpless, hopeless, powerless beings.

I don't like being told that I represent disabled people, because I *don't*. I represent myself. Some of what I do may ricochet around and benefit others, but I can't do it *for* them. They have to do it for themselves.

I don't see myself as a crusader. I just see myself as a person who has problems in certain areas and who has learned how to get over them.

12

Mark's Story

My father is a priest in a church in Wales and I come from a close-knit, caring Christian family. I was brought up largely in a very rural environment, a little country parish called Beguildy in mid-Powys, where my father was the local vicar running three churches. My earliest childhood memories are of living in what seemed to me then a very large Victorian mansion with huge gardens full of trees. The community was small and my father's position in it also gave *me* a certain status there, which was something that I learned to like a lot.

I have many happy recollections of traditional family Christmases: singing carols together around the tree, giving and receiving presents, going to church in the snow . . . My parents always seemed quite good at teaching me to develop and were supportive in terms of my education. There was also one particular teacher in my life, a man called Emrys Davies, who instilled in me a desire, a thirst, for knowledge when I was between the ages of nine and eleven. He was a very formative influence.

On reflection, there are three people who register in my life and who are important in terms of how I related initially to Alison.

The first one, Andrew, whom I met when I was younger,

greatly affected my perception of disabled people. Andrew was the disabled grandson of the church warden of one of Dad's churches and he had CP. My first meeting with him was very traumatic. He was about six or seven years older than I was and he wore big boots and his limbs seemed quite uncoordinated. When I asked him a question I couldn't understand what he said, and that may have been due to my own deepseated embarrassment, because I didn't know at that stage how to relate to him.

The other two were less influential. One was a little girl of about nine, the younger sister of a close friend of mine at school, who had spina bifida. I was eighteen and can remember being able to relate to her reasonably well. The second person was a guy called Andy, who was in college with me at Plymouth. Andy had a large lump on his back and obviously had great difficulty in walking, though I don't know the exact nature of his disability. He had no problem with communication, and he did his degree. He was an individual to whom I could relate, though there were differences in temperament between us. Andy was the studious, academic type, whereas the rest of us in the house we all shared were more frivolous and noisy — and that's where the tension lay.

It was Andrew who had the biggest impact on my thinking. Towards Emma (the little girl with spina bifida), I had adopted a 'Isn't she wonderful' attitude — not so much patronising as just the way one relates towards people who are younger. But Andrew frightened and upset me, because he made me feel embarrassed. Some of that embarrassment came to the surface when I first met Alison. It was those emotions that were being tapped into, because they were so deep and had been registered a long time ago.

All my earliest years until I left home were ones of conforming in the sense of turning up for church on Sunday and various church youth events which I attended.

I went away to college (the college of St Mark and John at Plymouth) to read geography, history and sociology. Like many young people away from home for the first time I went completely wild. I got involved in drugs and alcohol. I lived a promiscuous lifestyle and generally abused myself for that whole period.

During my first year I still attended church on Sunday morning, never really knowing why and with an ever-increasing hangover after playing rugby, which was a big part of my life at college. (I was fixtures secretary of the rugby club.)

In my second year I lived with a girl, Megan, for about six months. I was utterly in love, or thought I was. But the relationship with Megan didn't work out, and ended over the summer holiday period. I came back to college in September and for that term lived it up, got drunk, smoked dope. It was a process of blocking myself out. I didn't want to be alone with myself.

At the same time I bumped into Megan again and she said she'd become a Christian, having had some sort of 'charismatic conversion' experience . . . and so I started going to church once more. My relationship with Megan started to progress again, though given her 'conversion', in a different way from before. Church, for me, became much more heightened and meaningful.

But at some point she went off with somebody else, and I had to come to terms with this. The Christian and loving response if I genuinely loved Megan, was to let her go. I prayed about it that night, read a passage from the Bible, and went to sleep in a very peaceful way, which I believe was the peace of Jesus coming on me . . . and this had a very liberating effect.

The next morning, after morning prayer in the chapel, I went to see my college chaplain and I said: 'You know, I think I want to be a priest.' And he said: 'That's very strange, because I had a dream several nights ago where this is what I heard suggested.' We talked about it and I decided to inform my parents.

They came to Plymouth that weekend and I told Dad first, on his own. I sat him down and went through my whole chequered history. I talked it through with him, the whole bit . . . I needed to explain all that 'background' in order to come to some sort of awareness of what stage I was at then.

It was a form of confession, and a very sacramental experience for me. I felt very free afterwards. I'd offloaded a lot of guilt, which I'd been storing up for some time.

I don't think I'd ever seen my wild lifestyle as a form of rebellion. I just wanted to enjoy myself and I did, although I got myself into a right little mess because of it and ended up with only a third class degree.

Having told my father that I felt 'called' to the Ministry, I then contacted (at my father's suggestion) some people who are involved in the church selection process. As a first stage in this process I had to see Bishop Benjamin of Swansea and Brecon (who later conducted my wedding service), spelling out to him almost exactly the same story as I'd told my father.

The bishop told me to go and see the Warden of Ordinands, who is the person who looks after the ordinands (priests in training). 'Fine,' said the Warden, 'we'll put you in, first of all, for the diocesan selection panel, then the provincial one.'

I got through the diocesan panel without much difficulty. At the same time I started to look around for potential theological colleges. I looked at a fair cross-section and came across St Stephen's House which, to me, seemed to be training priests in a tradition which I could learn about and get to make my own — that is, the Catholic tradition.

At the same time as I was checking out colleges, I went to the provincial selection panel, who made an unconditional recommendation. Basically, they just said: 'Go and get trained.' I had three days of intensive questioning, with people examining and discussing my academic standards, pastoral skills and so on. I think my enthusiasm and the definite conviction that I had had a positive calling, carried me through. I'd already been accepted by St Stephen's House, with the provision that I did one year working in a parish.

A community placement came up in St Albans in 1983, with what was known as a 'root' group, run by the USPG (United Society for the Propagation of the Gospel). It was a self-financing project linked with their home mission, where groups of young Christians live and work in a parish — on this occasion for a period of twelve months. It was valuable experience and involved me in ten to twelve hours' formal youth work each week, which I enjoyed and considered part of my calling. I also did general parish visiting, and I took a job in a pub to support myself.

I shared a flat with David, who was training to be a Methodist minister. David was as opposite to me as it's possible to be. He was very very skinny, and extremely shy. At that time he had no ability to project his personality to others, and because we were such a contrast, this was a source of great amusement to everybody at the Abbey and all those who knew us. I'm sure he has developed a lot since then.

One important event that year was my Stage Two certificate — and that was how I met Alison. We met during the first residential weekend at London Colney. There were, as I recall, several other disabled people. I didn't go out of my way to meet people with disabilities. I found them a bit difficult because I had been conditioned to see nothing except the outward wobble.

I think Alison was 'put up' by one of her friends to approach me. I was conscious of trying to be cool and normal, as if nobody out of the ordinary was talking to me, but being very aware of her disability.

That was the only contact I had with Alison at that stage. She registered, but no more than that.

We went on our separate ways for the next twenty weeks. Then, the second weekend came round. One thing that flashed through my mind when I saw Alison there, was: 'This is someone who's been planted here to see how we react — to observe us.' In the first session that weekend we all started laughing. Alison has a very infectious laugh, which she uses at times to defuse situations — and I think she was using it then. There was a lot of joking and hilarity.

We had several tasks to do as a group. We were randomly put together and our group functioned very well. We were quite compassionate people but with strong personalities. The youth workers running the weekend training manipulated that and deliberately put us in stressful situations.

As a result, Alison and I knew how we worked together. We didn't know much about each other, but we learned a lot about how we functioned under stress and things like that. And from that moment she had made a strong impression not only to me, but on others in the group . . . though *my* feelings were running deeper.

By this time I was less aware of the wobbles, but the disability itself fascinated me, and I found it interesting talking to Alison about that and learning from her own experiences of disability.

When the weekend came to an end, we were all kissing each other goodbye and I kissed Alison on the forehead — I remember that quite clearly. So, for me, there was still quite a lot of prejudice and embarrassment to overcome.

After we left, our group decided to hold a reunion about a

month later. We got together and organised a disco in the crypt underneath St Albans Abbey and we proceeded to get quite drunk. When I'd had enough to slow up my inhibitions I started dancing with Ally — close dancing. The party broke up after the chaplain at the Abbey, a close friend of mine (Father Robbie) phoned the crypt and said that as *he* could hear the din we were making and lived further away than the Dean did, we would be pretty certain to wake the Dean if we didn't wrap things up fairly quickly.

So we all went back to my flat and carried on the party there. Somehow Alison and I ended up alone together in my bedroom, and I remember lines like: 'I really like you.' 'I like you too.' (I think it was me who said it first.) I suppose we were both trying to say: 'I love you.' We talked most of the night, and we fell asleep with others in my room.

We saw each other twice more that week and things were developing quite deeply by then, though I was still having problems accepting Alison's disability. I remember phoning my best friend Duncan, who said to me: 'Don't have anything to do with a spastic. You'll have to care for her for the rest of your life.' However, after he met her, he did say he thought there was a lot of potential in the relationship, as we would never stop learning from one another about what it was like to be 'normal' or 'disabled'. And that *is* a continuing process for both of us.

Towards the end of August 1984, after I had rounded up my affairs in St Albans, Ally came back to Builth for two weeks with my brother Simon and me. The car was packed with all my belongings. We broke down just outside Reading and had to be towed home. Mum rushed out to the car and kind of *smothered* Ally, almost carrying her into the house. I think both Dad and Mum had problems at that stage in accepting our relationship.

Then, as I recall, I came back to Watford with Alison and

stayed with her in the flat for week or so before starting at St Stephen's House in September. This was the first time she had been left on her own in the flat, without me, since I returned from France the previous month. So this was Ray's big chance to come back on the scene.

The following weekend I came back to see her on the Friday night, returning on the Saturday evening, and that was when I discovered he'd sprayed 'Holy Bastard' in cellulose paint on the boot of my car. I showed it to the Principal, who said: 'Perhaps you ought to leave it quite steady with this girl?'

I was incredulous and couldn't get over the *hostility*. I think Ray really was in love with her, but he never learned the lesson that I hope *I* learned with Megan: that if you do love somebody a lot, the most loving thing you can do in that situation is to leave well alone.

I can understand a little how he must have felt. *I* felt like going to chuck bricks through his window, but I'm quite tolerant in many ways, and this incident has become the source of a joke because the car wasn't very new (an old Avenger), so it didn't matter too much.

It was the best thing Ray ever did because Alison went up and wiped the floor with him, and that was it. Sometimes it's possible to finish a relationship and still remain friends, though it doesn't often happen.

After that, I knew I was on a winning wicket. Alison became a regular fixture at St Stephen's House, well known and liked by most of the people there — accepted as Alison, Mark's girlfriend, but in the end, much more as Alison in her own right, as part of the college community.

Gradually, our relationship deepened. We also went through ups and downs. At one point my parents had a real go at me about our relationship. Their main concern was that Alison was not a practising Christian, but that objection ceased when she was confirmed by the Archbishop of Wales at St Stephen's House in June 1986. Alison had met him the previous summer, and he happened to be coming to St Stephen's House to preach. I remember Alison's crystal-clear responses echoing out.

Once she was confirmed and a communicant, nothing more was said. I can't speak for them as to whether or not there ever was some prejudice. I suspect that there might have been. I suspect that now, today, they are thoroughly thrilled by all the media attention and success that Alison is attracting. My father seems to have warmed to Ally progressively. When he took her out to a formal dinner at the Royal Welsh Show, I think he loved very minute of it. The Royal Welsh Show is run by the Royal Welsh Agricultural Society in Builth Wells. It takes place over four days each year and is a huge spectacle of a show, drawing thousands of people from all over Wales, who come there to find out about agriculture. There are vast livestock displays, various types of farm machinery.

The dinner is quite a posh affair, frequented by members of the aristocracy. My father rather enjoyed the fact that his daughter-in-law was a *celebrity*. He was basking in a bit of that reflected glory, as all her friends do and probably myself to the greatest extent. That has probably led to an enormous level of acceptance right across the family now.

All three of my brothers have accepted Alison. My brother Simon met and accepted her early on. When I came back to St Albans from France I brought him back with me for a couple of weeks. Simon was then about seventeen. In my usual way I had built up Alison to be some kind of monster. I knew he would have to be really cool, or else she would go: 'What's the matter with you? Why are you taking the mickey out of my disability?' — which is how she was when I first met her: aggressive, defensive, over that sort of thing.

I went to work in the pub, leaving Simon in the flat so that when Alison came round he had to look out the window for her to let her in. He adjusted much more quickly than I had and after meeting her said something like: 'You've got a good one here, Mark. Hang on to this one — much better than all the others.'

I don't believe I've lost any friends because of Alison. There might be personality clashes, but that's different. I've gained friends, because I've got a special wife and that has made me more interesting to people!

As for the attitude of society in general, I just thought: 'Sod the world. I'm going to marry Alison, because I love her.' Ultimately, that was the only thing that mattered.

I was quite heavily grilled by members of staff at St Stephen's House when I said I wanted to get married. (Technically, a priest in the Anglican Church has to ask for 'indulgences' to marry: it's just a formality.) I had other friends there who wished to marry and the staff paid lip service to their situation, but I was given a much stronger grilling. The Principal of the House did it in a nice, very caring way, and when I explained how independent Alison was, he was very understanding. I don't think it had occurred to him that she drove to college to see me, or that she lived alone in her own flat.

My personal tutor was very supportive, especially during the stage just prior to our wedding, when I felt that both sets of parents were causing us difficulties: the usual mundane quibbles about where the wedding would be and when, who would pay for what. There were other tensions, internal family dynamics, which caused problems, and I felt that Father Brian Curnew (my personal tutor) more than any other member of staff, thought the marriage was *right* and was willing to help us in any way he could. He was also the only member of staff whom I asked to concelebrate at our nuptial mass.

One senior member of staff was aggressively against my marrying Alison. On one occasion he took me aside and implied that she would be a millstone around my ministry — that I'd be spending so much time caring for her that I could not be effective in the parish.

This made me very cross, and when Alison and I thought about it afterwards it made us both cry. I was shocked that somebody who was a priest in the Christian Church could behave in that way. It really did upset me — and it still *grates* a little when I think about it today.

But we did get married — and we got married because we love each other, and that's the important thing.

Once I had made the decision to be ordained I was convinced that I would have no more sexual relationships until I married. Then Alison came along, and we only got beyond stage one because she was attracted to me as much as I was to her. Once I'd come through that level of attraction and intimacy, then all the rest — my previous fears and worries — seemed quite stupid afterwards.

I think I was probably a great disappointment to her to start with because I was so worried about whether I could kiss her properly and things like that, but once I was over that stage there was no problem.

In the Church's eyes sex before marriage is wrong, but we don't live in an ideal world and things can never conform to neat little codes and rules, however much we'd like them to and however convenient it would be. Life isn't like that.

Alison is lucky enough to be one of those people who found it easy to say No until the right person came along. *I* wasn't, and I made a mess of my life for that reason. The difficulty is that when you remove the taboos about it all, when you say: 'You can sleep with whoever you like,' the result is anarchy and a gross abuse of people — and the opposite of love is what comes out of it.

If anyone had suggested that I married Alison out of a sense of altruism, or pity, I would have been quite offended. I guess that the Principal and others at St Stephen's House might have thought that was a motive, but people who know me well realise that I would never have gone ahead with the marriage for that reason.

I have always been rather unpredictable. My becoming a priest was in itself a big surprise for many people, and I don't believe that my marrying Alison was any greater a surprise.

I was ordained in June 1987 to the diaconate of St Albans Treboeth, Swansea, and immediately took up residence there the night after my ordination. After our wedding and brief honeymoon, Alison joined me there. She is very supportive, an asset in the parish, because I think she actually believes in the work I am doing. This may not be in the spiritual sense (her faith has not yet developed very much), but she can understand that my role is important when I'm working with young people and when I'm dealing with people in bereaved situations.

When I first met Alison, she had vehemently anti-religious beliefs. We coped with this through rows, arguments. I found it really hard, because I couldn't communicate to her all the love and peace which *I* had experienced. Why could I not make her understand?

Her level of acceptance depends on the mood she is in. Sometimes she is caustically against the Church; at other times she thinks quite deeply about it. All I could, and would, ask of her is that she is open and receptive, and then I'm sure something *will* happen. It's an inevitable process in the position she is in.

I like to think that I gave Alison the support and back-up she needed when she went to college to do her youth and community certificate. I like to feel that I added a little bit of comfort along the way, compared with her previous boyfriend, who was fairly set in his ways and who saw a woman's primary function as provider in the home.

My expectations of marriage are very much of somebody who is alongside me as my partner in life, and I see Alison as somebody who has an equal share in this relationship. At the moment she is developing her potential and fighting against the able-bodied world in that way. I think getting married was a part of that.

Right now she just seems to be getting better and better. Once we get into our fifties and sixties perhaps she will slow down quicker than I will, but that's too far off yet to contemplate.

I think we probably will have a family, though we enjoy life's creature comforts and these would be knocked if we did. Certain forms of disability are genetic; others, like CP, are not. There might be a difficulty (physically) with Alison having a baby. If there is, that's the most certain reason why we *will* have one, because Alison likes to prove *everything*. I think she would even go so far as to put her life on the line for it if she felt that was proving a point.

There are times when I just have to sit back and watch her struggle, however painful that might be. Sometimes, if we are in a hurry, I will do up her shoe laces: that's a concession she will accept. I always do her earrings as well. You do learn pretty quickly with Ally when to offer help and when to leave her to battle on.

I think Alison is somebody who doesn't make many friends. People will be friendly with her, but she won't call *them* friends. I'm the opposite. Alison is much more reserved than I am, because making friends makes her feel vulnerable. She's very vulnerable to *me* and that will result in hostility at times, as I can hurt her. We are both strong personalities and there are clashes because of that. There aren't many people who can get underneath and hurt her. She's very resilient and won't let them through. She's open and frank, but there's a barrier. I broke that barrier down. I think she still finds that hard: the fact that I probably know her better, more completely, than anybody — even her parents.

It's interesting — I love the *whole person* of Alison. *She* doesn't love her disability. She hates it. In a way, she's got to (hate it). It's only hating the 'spastic' that has made her push on, to beat that 'spastic' and in a way obliterate it.

I find her whole personality attractive. I find her good looking as well. Defining looks is a very subjective affair, but I find Alison sexually attractive in that way. I suppose a lot of this is because I no longer notice the wobbles, the funny facial expressions, the slurring of her speech. I don't see any of that. I actually see much more of *Alison*.